VICTORIAN TRUE SHORT STORIES
from the
WHITEHERN ARCHIVES

VICTORIAN TRUE SHORT STORIES *from the* WHITEHERN ARCHIVES

Mary J. Anderson, PhD

Rock's Mills Press
Oakville, Ontario
2019

ACKNOWLEDGEMENTS

I would like to acknowledge my daughter and her husband's help throughout: Janelle (Anderson) Baldwin, M.A. and Paul Baldwin; also George Down for the fine job he did for the editing; also David Stover and Rock's Mills Press for assistance in publishing. I am also grateful to Tom Minnes, curator, and the staff at Whitehern Historic House and Garden; and to the Hamilton Public Library for providing space and technical expertise for the continuing maintenance of the Whitehern Museum website: www.whitehern.ca. Also, my good friends Lori Goldblatt and Rebecca Orr have encouraged me throughout.

Published by
Rock's Mills Press
www.rocksmillspress.com

Copyright © 2019 by Mary J. Anderson.
All rights reserved. Published by arrangement with the author.

No part of this publication may be reproduced or transmitted, in any form or by any means, without the permission of the publisher. For information, contact us at customer.service@rocksmillspress.com.

CONTENTS

Introduction ... 3

[Rev.] Thomas Baker and the War of 1812 ... 8

Marriage to a Dead Sister's Husband—Unlawful!? ... 13

Rev. Thomas Baker's Daughter-in-Law: Mary Mudge Baker, Who *"Knew of Only One Way to Augment Her Income"* ... 20

Rev. Thomas Baker and Women's Rights ... 25

Mary Baker's Wedding to Isaac Baldwin McQuesten: June 18, 1873 ... 26

The Children of Isaac and Mary ... 31

The Wedding of Rev. Thomas Baker's Granddaughter, Alice Baker, to Edward Harbin ... 33

Dr. Calvin McQuesten, The Industrial Tycoon (1801–1885) ... 35

Elizabeth Fuller McQuesten, "The Wicked Stepmother" ... 39

Hilda-Belle's Thwarted Romance ... 41

Thomas Baker McQuesten's Thwarted Romance ... 44

[Rev.] Calvin McQuesten: Disabled Left Hand, Mental Fragility and Faith Healing ... 46

Address by Rev. Calvin McQuesten to the Hamilton Parks Board ... 51

World War One, 1914 to 1918 ... 54

Dr. Norman Victor Leslie Writes from the Trenches in World War One: *What War Really Means I Know Now* ... 56

Ruby Baker McQuesten:
Ruby's Tragic Life Story and Thwarted Romance ... 63

The Rebellion of Upper Canada, December 7, 1837:
William Lyon Mackenzie and Sir Isaac Buchanan ... 71

Victorian Medicine:
Lottie Baker's Cleft Palate and Surgery ... 74

Victorian Medicine: Diabetes and Heroic Medicine ... 91

Victorian Medicine: Women's Health and Education ... 95

Calomel: A Mercury Compound ... 99

Margaret Edna McQuesten: Mental Illness ... 102

Victorian Medicine:
Isaac McQuesten and the "Aristocratic Vice" ... 105

Dr. Calvin Brooks McQuesten:
Alexandra Arcade and Bequest to Mary P. ... 112

The Hamilton Club and Whitehern ... 114

Medical Student Letters While Travelling Abroad
and Studying in Europe ... 118

The Memorial Arch at Niagara Falls—and Peace ... 136

The Big Bell Fiasco: The Carillon Controversy ... 141

The City Beautiful and Peace ... 144

"The Forgotten Builder" and Partisan Politics ... 155

VICTORIAN TRUE SHORT STORIES
from the
WHITEHERN ARCHIVES

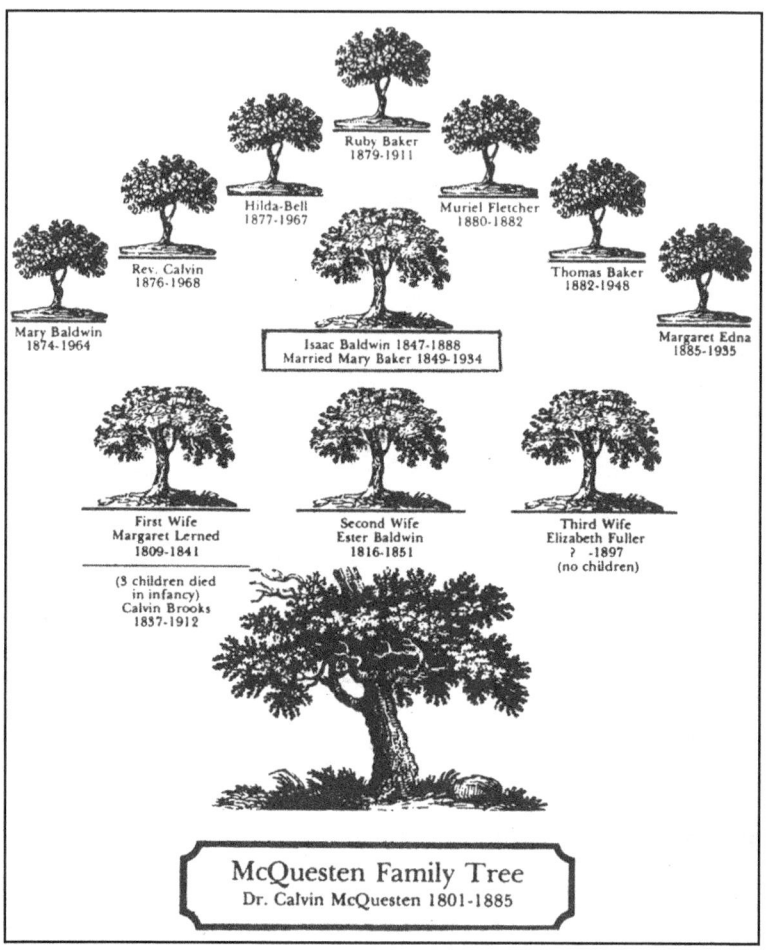

INTRODUCTION

There are many Victorian stories in the Whitehern Archives; they cover the subjects of family, history, war, romance, and medicine. The true stories in this volume have been selected and compiled from the thousands of personal letters that are extant and preserved at Whitehern Museum and are also available in a digitized form at www.whitehern.ca. The square-bracketed numbers added here in the text refer to the letters being used, and they can be consulted through the Whitehern website for expansion or clarification. They have all been transcribed.

For these writings we are using "Victorian" to relate to the Victorian sensibility and ideals in Canada that outlasted the life and death of Queen Victoria (1819–1901). In fact, Whitehern and the McQuestens carried on some traditions that have long been lost. For instance, the organ controversy raged in the MacNab Street Presbyterian Church for many years, from 1850 to 1900, as the congregation argued vehemently against an organ as: "a prophanation [*sic*] of a place of worship," an "instrument of Satan" and a "kist o' Whistles," partly because they saw it as "entertainment." They hung on to traditions that we might find ludicrous today. They finally accepted the organ, but Mary McQuesten still did not like it because she found it was too loud. She preferred the Precentor who used a tuning fork to lead the singing in the Psalms—hymns were not permitted. Mary also objected to the bells at St. Paul's Church because they were so noisy. Dancing was condemned and forbidden [W5508; W5172]. Revival meetings were favoured: *the two noted Evangelists T & A [Torrey and Alexander] were coming to the city, they had done a great work etc., etc.… [they] denounce evil in a way most refreshing & wholesome* [W5508]. Many of these letters are full of gossip because they viewed gossip as "neighbours' watchfulness," and gossip was reported at the regular church meetings. We would find it very awkward today to conform to these and other Victorian ideals [W-MCP3-5.011 Fn3].

The letters on the Whitehern website were written mostly by and to the extended McQuesten and Baker families from 1812 until 1968. Whitehern is the name of the McQuesten family home, formerly Willowbank, at 41 Jackson St., Hamilton, Ontario. It is now a museum and a Canadian Heritage site; and is unique in that it displays all of the original family possessions just as they were used by the family members from 1852, when Dr. Calvin McQuesten purchased and moved into the home, until 1968, when the last remaining McQuesten family member died: Rev. Calvin McQuesten, at the age of ninety-two. He and his two sisters, Mary and Hilda, lived at Whitehern into their nineties and, as is evidenced by the extant letters, in their senior years they lived lives of "quiet desperation." They often did not agree with one another—partly because Rev. Calvin McQuesten had become a United Church minister, rather than Presbyterian. However, they all had a strong sense of history. They were also very proud of their sibling, The Hon. Thomas Baker McQuesten, MPP (1882–1948), and what he had accomplished for Hamilton, for Niagara, and for all of Ontario.

Many of the letters on the website were brought into the house by the McQuesten family from their former homes, some from New Hampshire. These letters have been transcribed and digitized and may be read and researched on the website, as noted above. However, for this writing we have sorted and categorized the letters into themes and stories in order to inform and pique the curiosity of the reader into the Victorian conscience, and to encourage research and a further perusal of the website.

The search mechanism on the website works very well by typing a name, letter number, city, word or phrase, into the search box in the upper right-hand corner when on the site and selecting from the list provided. In most cases the first documents or letters displayed are the most relevant to the search query.

We are grateful to Mary Farmer, a retired Hamilton librarian, who first rescued the Whitehern letters from the basement of Hamilton City Hall. They had languished there in boxes ever since 1968, following the death of Rev. Calvin McQuesten, when Whitehern was donated to the City of Hamilton to be used as a museum or "period piece." As time went on, it was feared that the letters may have been deposited there in preparation for casting into the furnace. We are also grateful to Mary Farmer for cataloguing a major portion of the letters and writing an introduction about each of the family members. This document she named *A Calendar of McQuesten Papers*; it is on file today at the Whitehern Historic House and Garden. Subsequently, Georgina Minnes, a Whitehern researcher, wrote a brief biography and history for each of the family members. The letter numbers quoted here are the numbers used in the Calendar, which we have designated as: **"Calendar of McQuesten Papers at Whitehern" (CMQPW)**. Some of the numbers are those on the microfilm at Whitehern and the microfilm numbers begin with W-MCP#etc. Many of the microfilmed letters are digitized and on site also.

Queen Victoria reigned from 1837 to 1901 and was a revered monarch in Canada. She was considered a symbol of ideal womanhood. After her death, women in Hamilton raised the money to erect a statue to Queen Victoria which stands in Gore Park today in the centre of the city. The MacNab Street Presbyterian Church (which was the McQuesten family's church) and other religious establishments assisted in prolonging Victorian views and ideals. The inscriptions on the statue are a tribute to Queen Victoria's enduring influence and her role as a model for women. The inscriptions read:

Queen Victoria statue in Gore Park in Hamilton (Courtesy Google)

QUEEN VICTORIA, QUEEN AND EMPRESS, A MODEL WIFE & MOTHER.

Below the lion at her feet are the words:

MANY CHILDREN OF OUR CHILDREN SAY SHE WROUGHT HER PEOPLE LASTING GOOD.

Mary McQuesten comments on the statue and the lion: *The great event for that day is the unveiling of the Queen's statue. All we are able to see now is the old lion lying at the base. He is a fine fellow and it seems to me very true to nature, not the time honoured one which appears with the unicorn and is really much handsomer, but like the beast in its natural state as I remember seeing it in Central Park. This one is in green bronze and reclines against the flag, its head raised as if watching.*

HISTORY

Dr. Calvin McQuesten

Calvin Brooks McQuesten

(left to right) Hilda, Tom, Mary, Mary (Jr.) Edna, Ruby, Calvin
(C. 1890)

Rev. Thomas Baker

Isaac B. McQuesten

Victorian True Short Stories from the Whitehern Archives

Women's Foreign Missionary Society, 1897

*Mary Baker McQuesten as President
(right foreground, see arrow)
Inscription reads: Twenty-first annual meeting, W.F.M.S. Of
the Presbyterian Church in Canada*

[REV.] THOMAS BAKER AND THE WAR OF 1812

We begin these "true stories" with [Rev.] Thomas Baker (1795–1887), Mary Baker McQuesten's father. This is not technically a Victorian story, since it deals with an era before Queen Victoria, whose reign began June 20, 1837. We might not normally expect to have letters at Whitehern as old as dating from the War of 1812, but the grandfather at Whitehern, Rev. Thomas Baker, actually served in the War of 1812 *in Canada* before he went back to England to train as a minister, and then returned to Canada. When Rev. Thomas Baker became aged, he lived at Whitehern and died there. Many of Baker's letters are extant on the website and in Mary Farmer's Calendar. Farmer states, in her introduction, that Rev. Thomas Baker is *one of the noblest characters* among the letters, since he arranged to finance his grandchildren's care and education after their father and mother died, and when they were left with a stepmother with questionable morals. As we can see by the letters and the stories, Rev. Baker is a little less than noble in some regards. He demonstrates a rigid Calvinistic patriarchal religious sensibility that was not shared by all clergy and that has now been largely lost.

Thomas Baker was the son of a sea captain in the British Merchant Marine. He enlisted in the Navy at the age of 11 and went to sea as a midshipman. He served on several ships and received his training and education in the navy. He served during the Napoleonic Wars and received several promotions. He came to Canada from Portsea, England, and served in the British Navy there during the War of 1812.

Baker was sent to Canada at the request of Captain James Lucas Yeo, who wrote to England from Kingston, Ontario, during the War of 1812, requesting some trained midshipmen capable of serving as officers. His letter states: *I likewise request your Lordship will send me a good set of active young men as midshipmen who have passed for lieutenants. They are in this service a most useful class of officer* [W8714, Footnote 2].

It is as a result of this letter that Thomas Baker (later Reverend, and father of Mary Baker McQuesten) joined the crew of the HMS *St. Lawrence* as a midshipman. The newly-built ship weighed 3200 tons, had 120 guns, and sailed out of Kingston, Ontario. When it was launched from there on October 15, 1814, under Commander-in-Chief Sir James Yeo, the American ships immediately recognized its might and never challenged it. Thus, the HMS *St. Lawrence* with Thomas Baker on board actually won the War of 1812 on Lake Ontario and did so without having to fire a cannon.

HMS St. Lawrence, Thomas Baker's ship during war of 1812 (Courtesy Google)

Thomas Baker received his Lieutenant's commission in 1815. In 1817 he withdrew from active service and went back to England to train for the ministry in the Congregational Church. When he retired at Whitehern in 1870 at age 75, he was granted a pension of eight shillings per day concurrent with his promotion to Commander in H.M. Fleet.

Thomas Baker trained for the ministry at the Theological College at Portsea, England, now Portsmouth. In 1819 he married Sarah Orange Hampson (1799–1847), and they had eight children between 1820 and 1830. An infant child died in 1832. In 1835, Baker immigrated to Canada to become the minister of the first Congregational Church in Upper Canada at Kingston.

His seven living children came with him. In 1847 his wife, Sarah Hampson Baker, died.

By that time his children were grown, the youngest being eighteen years of age.

In 1846, Baker continued his ministry when he moved his family to Brantford, Ontario, and there are many interesting letters about his work there. Rev. Baker was a strict Calvinist disciplinarian and eventually resigned in indignation because the church members had not fulfilled their commitment to build a proper church. They had promised *to erect a comfortable and commodious place of worship* [W4126].

In 1848, Rev. Baker married for the second time, to Mary-Jane McIlwaine (1809/10–1882), and they had a daughter, Mary-Jane Baker (1849–1934) (name later changed to Mary). Mary-Jane was born in Brantford, Ontario, and was the beloved child of a late marriage—Baker was 54 and his wife was 40 at the time of Mary-Jane's birth. Rev. Baker and his wife doted on her because she was beautiful, intelligent and showed great potential.

The Baker family lived in Newmarket and they sent Mary to school in Toronto, to Mrs. Dr. Burns' Ladies' College. When Mary graduated from this school she returned home to Newmarket. Rev. Baker notes Mary's potential as he states: *My daughter, what shall we do with you in poor little out of the world Newmarket, after four terms residence in Toronto with such opportunities for pleasure and instruction? You must for a time reconcile yourself to circumstances, seek after self improvement. All that you have yet acquired only places you on the threshold of the temple of wisdom, has only given you some ability to tread the path of science* [W3004]. Baker also commented on Mary's ability in Italian and was looking forward to having her read to him.

Rev. & Mrs. Baker and daughter Mary-Jane Baker (Courtesy Whitehern)

Rev. Baker's daughter became Mary Baker McQuesten when she married Isaac McQuesten on June 18, 1873, and she eventually became the "Matriarch" of Whitehern. Her story is told in my first book, which is noted on the website:

The Life Writings of Mary Baker McQuesten: Victorian Matriarch (WLUP, 2004). (My second book is *Tragedy and Triumph: Ruby and Thomas B. McQuesten* [Tierceron Press, 2011].)

There can be little doubt that Rev. Baker's instruction to his daughter Mary helped to prepare her for the matriarchal role she was to play for the rest of her life with her own six living children and with the women's branch of the Presbyterian Church, both locally and provincially: the *Woman's Foreign Missionary Society,* and the *Women's Missionary Society* (*WFMS, WMS*). In her writings, Mary displays her father's deep religious sense and her belief in a personal and loving God who guides her every decision; although she comes to a modicum of doubt about her actions and His guidance as time goes on. Georgina Minnes, a Whitehern researcher, states that:

> *Mary's opinions are as firm and un-negotiable as were the laws of the Meads and Persians ... she had a real and puritanical sense of right and wrong ... an uncompromising conscience ... [and] inflexible integrity* [CMQPW p.14].

Mary Baker McQuesten bore seven children in fourteen years. Her husband died very suddenly in 1888. He died bankrupt as the result of business failure, and of alcoholism and various addictions. He had also suffered from mental illness, for which he was receiving regular treatment. It was impossible to quell the suspicions that Isaac's sudden death was a suicide; however, the family did not speak or write of these suspicions, and Isaac received an honourable, religious, and public funeral.

In Isaac's letter to his half-brother, Dr. Calvin Brooks McQuesten in New York, he writes about his treatment for mental disorders at Homewood Sanatorium in Guelph with Dr. Lett [W2511, October 1, 1887]. He describes his symptoms and habits: addictions, "temptations" and "stimulants." He also makes some puzzling remarks to his brother to alert him to a mysterious plan, and to be *prepared to act quietly and calmly, when, and if, it becomes necessary to act* [W2511]. There is more about Isaac and his addictions in one of the final chapters of this work, under the heading "Victorian Medicine."

By the time that Mary-Jane Baker was born and going to school, the seven living children of Rev. Baker's first marriage were grown; some had married and had children of their own. It is these grandchildren whom Baker seeks to rescue when he learns that their morals are in danger of becoming corrupted by their stepmother's questionable behaviour and influence and, in one case, by marriage to a dead sister's husband.

Rev. Thomas Baker (courtesy Whitehern)

MARRIAGE TO A DEAD SISTER'S HUSBAND—UNLAWFUL!?

Many years after the death of his first wife, Rev. Baker had troubles with his first family and with his grandchildren. His letters record that in 1847 he became greatly alarmed about the relations between Mary-Anne (1828–1850), his third daughter, and her brother-in-law, Frederick F. Wilkes, the widowed husband of her deceased sister Harriet (who had died in childbirth in 1847). At the time, Baker believed that this kind of family relationship was decreed to be against the civil law and against the church law which Baker upheld. Rev. Baker did his utmost to save his *poor, misguided, motherless child from the improper course she has been pursuing* [W2864, June 6, 1848].

Rev. Baker writes a very strong letter to Wilkes: *With deep anguish of soul I inform you that I have heard from several of my friends that your **criminal passion** for your deceased wife's sister had been suspected and was talked of with **loathing and disgust**. Pray that God, who has mercifully saved my child from degradation and misery, affect your heart to feel the sinfulness of your conduct, and give you ... repentance for having laboured to teach a daughter to disregard the wishes and authority of, unhappily now, her sole parent in order that she might become the victim of your **incestuous lust**. The activity of which you endeavoured to conceal from her mind by proffering marriage and thus induce to the commission of crime forbidden by God and abhorred by man. May the Lord cause you to feel it thus. Can it be possible that you do not see it thus? If you do not may He enlighten your understanding that you may **loathe yourself** on account of your mistaken conduct?* [W2931, emphasis added].

However, Wilkes and Mary-Anne did marry, and Rev. Baker disowned her and refused to see her. Mary-Anne (Baker) Wilkes died in childbirth in 1850. Her father Rev. Thomas Baker had refused to see her as she begged for his forgiveness on her deathbed. Her "sin" was that she had married Frederick F. Wilkes against her father's wishes. For some people at that time, marriage to a deceased wife's sister was unlawful.

Rev. Baker warns Mary-Anne, in a letter on August 18, 1848 [W2880] from Brantford. He addresses it: *My all but ruined child, I yesterday was informed and today the report was confirmed, that recently in Montreal a case of marriage with a deceased wife's sister was tried before Judge Day. It was [a case?] of considerable interest as large property was depending. The learned Judge decided that the Law of The Land was the Law in Canada consequently the marriage was illegal and the children being thereby illegitimate could not inherit. My dear Mary, you are on the brink of a precipice – a step and you are gone. May God in his mercy save you from irretrievable ruin fervently pray. Your unhappy Father, Thomas Baker.*

Rev. Baker's legalistic nature is also evident in the fact that he notes that he has retained, *a true copy of the original.* This is so that he would have a copy of the letter for his files, and it is this copy that we have in the archive.

Baker refused to see his daughter thereafter. Mary-Anne took shelter at her friends, the Walkers, who consulted a lawyer, Samuel Black Freeman, to determine what rights Mary-Anne had to choose either her own residence or marriage partner. They found that the law gave Mary-Anne, who was then approximately 19 or 20 years of age, the right to choose both [W2855, May 3, 1848 & footnote]. The lawyer had given his ruling to Walker, that if the child was of age then she could choose her own residence [W2851, April 24, 1848]. However, this did not satisfy her father, and he accuses his daughter of **prostitution** and **harlotry** *because she married her dead sister's husband:* [W2870, July 11, 1848, footnote] he *would urge* his daughter *prior to her becoming the Liaison of her brother in law to stipulate for the price of her prostitution: so that should he at any time please to dismiss her she may receive the hire* [payment] *of a **harlot** and depart without murmuring* [emphasis added]. After making these abusive remarks, Rev. Thomas Baker continued to refuse to see Mary-Anne. See also W2855 for details, footnote and links.

In W2855, when Mary-Anne had unexpectedly arrived at the home of Mr. James Walker (in April of 1848), Walker wrote to her father. As a result of what Samuel Black Freeman had told them, the

Walkers gave Mary-Anne shelter in their home and refused to send her back to her father, instead asking that her clothes and books be returned so that she could complete her education. Outraged, Rev. Baker refused to comply with the request, asserting his "inalienable right ... of choosing her [Mary-Anne's] residence" [W2856]. Many of Rev. Baker's letters to Mary-Anne have an authoritarian and manipulative character, typically condemning her relationship to Wilkes as "prostitution" [W2870] and with a tone of bitter condemnation and haughty religious fervour; then suddenly softening with promises of a father's love and forgiveness if she rejected the "marriage settlement" and came home.

On July 1, 1848, Mary-Anne writes a very strong letter to her father:

[W2868, July 1, 1848] TO REV. THOMAS BAKER FROM HIS DAUGHTER MARY-ANNE BAKER, HAMILTON, ONTARIO

My dear papa, I received about three weeks ago, a letter from yourself, and yesterday one from John [likely, her brother John Orange Baker]; *in both which letters, many terms of a very uncalled for, and offensive kind, were used towards very kind and dear friends.*

From the spirit of these letters, it is very evident, that if from any considerations, I declined to become Frederic's wife, a home in my own family, is quite out of the question.

My dear pa; allow me to say, that in leaving my Brother's house, I was guided by my own voluntary wish. In so doing to escape from unjust, and uncalled for confinement was my sole object. In my stay with my dear, and faithful friends, (Mr. and Mrs. Walker) I have even received the kind sympathy of devoted friendship. Is not their house (next to your own) the one, which six months ago, you would have chosen as a home for me & surely in so short a time, they cannot have changed to such a degree, as to deserve all the abusive epithets, which they have received, and of all the unkind reflections, which have been so literally bestowed by my own family, those contained in John's letter of the 30th inst. appear to be the most unworthy.

I shall not in future desire to receive letters from my friends, with the last two as specimens of their spirit; whilst I shall still ever bear towards those whose blood runs in my veins, a deep and anxious interest in my heart.

Believe me my dear pa, I deeply sympathize with you in your painful illness, and were it pract'able would esteem it a duty and a privilege, to return to your house, to minister to your wants, and relieve your anxious mind, but with present feelings and under existing circumstances, it is impossible.

With sincere affection I remain, My dear papa, Yours etc., Mary Anne

In Baker's lengthy letter of response, following, we can see that he gives a rather conditional personal "forgiveness" to his daughter, but does NOT give her the religious "consolation" that she had pleaded for; and he closes his letter with a great deal of preaching.

[W2894, August 20, 1849] TO MARY-ANNE [BAKER] WILKES, FROM THOMAS BAKER, BRANTFORD [ONTARIO]

My dear Mary [Anne],

On Friday I was informed by Mrs. Kipps you wished to see me. Why she did not state. Is it, my child, that affliction has caused reflection that you now feel that you are verily guilty concerning your father. Then you wish to express to him your contrition and ask his forgiveness. If so I fully and freely forgive you.

[However] I am very sorry I cannot be with you to give you religious instruction and consolation. That I cannot have the melancholy privilege I had with dear Harriett. You must remember the solemn declaration I made you in the presence of Witness to deter you from doing what I foresaw would be replete with misery to us both. And though you may now wish me to disregard the engagement, I feel that it must be inviolably kept.

We can never, Mary, meet on earth. But we must be apart from each other. This is very painful, but it is the legitimate consequence of your own conduct. And I can only deplore what is not in my power to remedy ...

But why has God permitted this? Why have your pleasures been so

short lived? Have you asked these questions? I wish to render you the greatest service in my power and therefore would be faithful. Review the past, my child, twice you have professed to be under religious impressions and you have turn[ed] your back from God. It may be He is now making a last effort for your salvation. He is chastising you for your profit that He is now determined his gracious purpose shall be accomplished. That you shall hear and your soul shall live. Do you my dear child, face it with God's design. Think of the value of your soul. Do you think of its danger, do think of the provision which divine mercy has made for its salvation the willingness of Christ to save.

You may recover. Let not the hope of this induce procrastination and lull you with fatal security. Should you be restored, you must shortly die. Obey then I beseech you the word of our Lord which I spoke unto thee, and it shall be well with thee and thy soul shall live ... Yes, go to him, dear Mary, go with heartfelt contrition, ingenuous and with faith in his 'precious blood' and He will receive you.

And then, dear child, though we can never meet on earth we shall meet in heaven, shall meet your dear mother and sister. Do you wish to meet your father? Is affection for him again reviving in your bosom, Alas! That its revival should ever have been necessary, and that it should have been so long delayed. Well though late it affords a melancholy satisfaction to one, who, for you Mary, feels he must go sorrowing to the grave. Grant the only request he [now can?] ask of you, give yourself to Xt [Christ] go to Him ... Your affectionate and deeply sorrowing, father Thomas Baker.

Mary Ann (Baker) Wilkes died in childbirth in 1850. Her father Rev. Baker, refusing to see her even as she pleaded for his forgiveness on her deathbed, states that it *affords him a* **melancholy satisfaction** [emphasis added] to see her in such distress and dying. While the legality of *marriage to a deceased sister's husband* was at that time considered unlawful by some authorities, this is debatable depending upon the authority consulted. Baker chose to select the authority that condemned her, while others sought legal authorities who hold an opposite position.

Baker was criticized by members of his flock and by other ministers for his legalistic sternness in the rejection of his daughter's pleas, and for his accusations against Wilkes. In this regard, Rev. Baker can be considered less than "*noble*" in his rigidity, and certainly members of his congregation viewed him in this negative way. His congregation slandered him because of his refusal to see his daughter, and for his accusations against Wilkes. There is a series of letters which deal with the charge of *slander* against Baker by his congregation; however, Rev. Baker never relents from his intractable position.

An example of this is the following in the exchange of letters with Rev. Enoch Barker, the minister who succeeded Baker when he resigned or retired. The tone of Barker's letter is somewhat incredulous, and suggests that Rev. Enoch Barker still believes what he has heard repeated many times by members of the congregation.

[W2984, November 21, 1864] TO REV. THOMAS BAKER, NEWMARKET, ONTARIO, FROM REV. ENOCH BARKER, NEWMARKET, ONTARIO

Dear Sir, I was surprised a day or two ago to hear indirectly that you deny the report which I have never before had the slightest reason to doubt, having heard again and again but the one statement of the case, and this from those who had the best opportunities of knowing, some of them reckoned among your intimate friends and who still believe it; – viz. That you refused to go and see your daughter when she sought your forgiveness on her dying bed. If I have been thus led into error, I should like to be informed of it, that I may make such reparation as duty required for having been one of many to repeat it.

On the same authority I have also said that when a majority of the Brantford church once wished to hold a meeting, they found the door locked against them, either by yourself or with your concurrence. If one report be incorrect the other may also be; though I have hitherto never doubted their truth, believing as others do that you thought that you were doing your duty in both cases.

I am, Rev. Sir, yours sincerely, E. Barker [Enoch]

Rev. Baker replies in conclusion and with some vehemence to Rev. Enoch Barker:

[W2986, November 22, 1864] TO REV. ENOCH BARKER, NEWMARKET, ONTARIO, FROM, REV. THOMAS BAKER, NEWMARKET, ONTARIO
... *With reference to yours of the 29th, I regret to say that, in my opinion, it is verbose, involved, offensive, contradictory, and so very unsatisfactory that I cannot discredit the statements of the parties above named. ["parties" is crossed out].*

I am happy to repeat "Your conduct furnishes me with a complete refutation of the slander," which they allege to have been uttered by you. Concluding, with this, my correspondence on this unpleasant affair.

I am, Rev. Sir, yours with all due respect, Thomas Baker.

REV. THOMAS BAKER'S DAUGHTER-IN-LAW: MARIA MUDGE BAKER, WHO "*KNEW OF ONLY ONE WAY TO AUGMENT HER INCOME*"

Following is the first mention of Mrs. Mudge in the letters, as Rev. Baker writes to his daughter Mary Baker McQuesten: *I have no recollection whatever of Mrs. Mudge, though she may have heard me in the Paris school house. Many know me, of whom I have no knowledge (Of course). You could not help meeting Sarah Mudge, but I have no wish for intimacy with any of that family. If [Lottie?] calls you must be polite, but my [?] ended with [them?] with the funeral service for Mr. Graham. You will not mention any thing of this* [W3004].

James Alfred Baker (1825–1876) was Rev. Baker's favourite son and became a successful farmer. He married Charlotte Puckridge, who died in 1864 leaving him a widower with seven children. James Alfred, who had run into financial difficulties in 1864, lost hope after the death of his wife, and the farm went into failure.

James Alfred married for a second time, in 1869, to Maria Mudge, a widow who had one child of her own, Nellie. Maria Mudge Baker thus became the stepmother of James Alfred Baker's seven children. When James Alfred died in 1876, Maria Mudge Baker had a very difficult time financially. Rev. Baker, the grandfather, helped her with some income. It is these seven grandchildren whom Baker seeks to rescue when he hears that their morals are in danger of becoming corrupted by their new mother. The family was very poor and had nothing except what Rev. Baker could send them. Mary Farmer states: *the unfortunate Maria Mudge knew of only one way to augment her income (CMQPW, Farmer 12)*.

In 1878 it was reported to Rev. Baker by a watchful neighbour, Henry Hart, that Maria Mudge was entertaining men in her home for undue *lengths of time* and thus was causing a *scandal*. Baker becomes concerned about the moral conduct of Maria Mudge, and the possible moral effect on his grandchildren. Another of Baker's sons, John Puckridge Baker, also reported the scandal to Rev. Baker and, when Baker made inquiries of Henry Hart, Hart confirmed the rumour that male visitors go to the house and stay undue periods of time [W3155, W3156]. Here is Rev. Baker's letter to Henry Hart:

[W3155, February 19, 1878] FROM REV. BAKER, 3 BOLD STREET, HAMILTON, ONTARIO, TO HENRY HART, ESQ:

Dear Sir, permit me to state to you that last week my grandson J.P. [John Puckridge] Baker called on me and gave me a very ill report of affairs at Paris. He informed me that in consequence of male visitors to the residence of his stepmother, and their remaining undue lengths of time, suspicions had been exalted in the minds of the neighbours, that whisperings had followed and at length, the above had become so verily known and talked about as now to be a scandal. For confirmation of his statements he referred me to you, having conversed about it with you. You would do me a great favour by acquainting me with all you know concerning this to me very distressing affair. It haunts my day & disturbs my rest at night. Of course, all you may write is considered by me strictly confidential, and I hope all I may write to you will by you be so considered.

Should what I have heard be confirmed, I must withdraw the children from her care; but what to do with them I am greatly at loss to know. Were it not for Mrs. Baker's very feeble health I might bring them to our home; but were I to do it now it would be at the risk of her life, therefore I dare not do it.

If you in kind remembrance of their poor father would suggest any thing for my questions it should meet my grateful and careful consideration. With very kind regard to you & Mrs. Hart. I am dear Sir, yours in deep affection, Thomas Baker.

Subsequently, Rev. Baker writes to Maria and removes his financial aid. He arranges the children to be distributed into the care of others. Following is Baker's personal letter to Maria:

[W3230, June 5, 1878] TO MARIA [MUDGE] BAKER, PARIS, ONTARIO, FROM HER FATHER-IN-LAW REV. THOMAS BAKER, 3 BOLD STREET, HAMILTON, ONTARIO

Mrs. James A. [Alfred] Baker

It appears from your letters that all afsistance[1] for your, Nellie's and the support of my late son's children has been derived from me; except "some second-hand clothes ... obtained from your brother in the States." ... That those so nearly related to me should have been drefsed in garments manufactured from cast clothes so acquired is to me very distasteful, especially after having contributed, in my estimation, a sum sufficient, if judiciously applied, for all necefsary purposes.

Further, your economy would not in future enable you to keep your expenditure within your income: —and lastly, that there is very painful discord between you and the elder branches of the family, and that it has unhappily extended to the younger, so that there is presumably spectacle of a house divided against itself.

John Puckridge Baker informed me you had said: If you were clear of the children and had three or four boarders it would be better for you than they. I have no doubt but it would. And as I cannot wish you to sacrifice the interests of yourself and daughter for the advantage of my grandchildren, and am unable to remit the amount of pecuniary aid, you in a recent letter seemed to indicate, you would require, I have relieved you from the care of them. And that you may have time to make arrangements for the future without pecuniary embarrafsment, I enclose you a Cheque on the Bank of Hamilton for sixty dollars. For the future you must depend on your own friends and management: I can only look to the juniors of my grandchildren. Wishing you and Nellie the constant presence and blefsing of the Widow's God.

I am, dear Mrs. Alfred, yours, with all due respect and esteem, Thomas Baker.

P.S. Any Bank in Paris will cash the cheque on your paying a quarter of a dollar. I have included postage stamps to that amount.

1. Rev. Baker uses the archaic "fs" for "ss," which we have retained in this transcription to demonstrate an archaic Victorian custom of writing. In other letters we have substituted the "ss" to make the letters more easily readable. It bears noting that the flawless form and flourish of Baker's penmanship is also a reflection of his dated and fastidious nature. Baker made copies of his letters to keep for his own file, and it is these copies that we find extant in the archive.

Rev. Baker did what his stern Calvinist nature prescribed and immediately undertook the difficult task of separating his grandchildren from their stepmother, placing them in suitable quarters elsewhere, and/or providing for their education (CMQPW, 12). There are many letters between 1877 and 1881 describing these circumstances. For example, Rev. Baker places one child as an apprentice dressmaker; another, Maud, is sent to a relative in England. Alice marries Edward Harbin. One son, John P., graduates in medicine from the University of Toronto and practises on Manitoulin Island until his death in 1936. One of the granddaughters, Lottie, undergoes surgery for a cleft palate, and this will be dealt with in the chapter on "Victorian Medicine."

Further letters to Maria Mudge and many other Baker writings are available by a search on the website of the Whitehern Archives: **www.whitehern.ca.** The fate of Baker's grandchildren is also recorded as they were placed in homes more suitable to Rev. Baker's standards. Several of the children expressed regret at having to leave their stepmother, Maria Mudge Baker, and attested to her care of them and their gratitude to her and distress at having to leave her. Therefore, there is some evidence in the letters that Maria Mudge may have been maligned. Hattie writes: ... *No one in this world could be more anxious to have a family comfortable and appear respectable than Mother, she deprives herself of many things which she needs all for the sake of making us cheerful and comfortable ... I think she has more than her share of trouble and I often think if I were her I would be glad to die at any moment for I don't think writing could express the trouble and cares she has on her mind* [W3168, April 2, 1878].

Rev. Thomas Baker was a model of Calvinist rectitude in his pastoral dealings and he demanded a very high moral standard from his congregation. His letters demonstrate his patriarchal expectations regarding his congregation. For instance, in his letter of August 1841, to his congregation in Paris, Ontario, he tendered his resignation because they had not fulfilled their promise to erect: *a comfortable and commodious place of worship* [W4126].

That in this aspect you are behind every other Congregation of this denomination in this Province, you are the only people who have allowed a year to pass away without the effort required of you and which I was encouraged to expect when invited to become your Pastor. It was well known that I had pledged myself to leave if the measure was not carried out in the time proposed ... It must be obvious to you that the necessity of dissolving my connection has been forced upon me [W4126].

The chastising and judgmental tone of the letter justifies his stance with a legalistic thoroughness. Rev. Baker's writings also contain a lengthy account of dissension within the church which is significant for two reasons. First, it discloses that his subsequent ministry in Brantford was also riddled with discipline problems which he proceeded to rectify with the same stern measures. The lengthy account for the years 1841 to 1848 concludes that members were, *most pertinaciously adhering to their opinions,* and the matter was finally resolved in 1849 with *resolutions ... and names of church members expelled and suspended* [W4129, W4142]. It is evident from the form and content of these accounts that Rev. Baker was a highly principled and inflexible pastor and meted out disciplinary measures with an Old Testament justice and a military rigour.

REV. THOMAS BAKER AND WOMEN'S RIGHTS

Although Rev. Baker was rigidly patriarchal in dealing with his congregation, he also defended Women's Rights to participate in church meetings and church politics. His account relates that a member of the congregation *objected to females speaking in the church*. At the next meeting, one month later, Baker *spoke at some length to the right of females to take part in transacting church business, showing that their being forbidden to speak related to the Worshipping Assemblies and not to meetings for the transacting of church affairs.* In his lengthy sermonic reply, he quotes extensively from the New Testament (some of his quotation is in Latin), and then he abruptly concludes that he hopes he has now *set the matter to rest* [W4129e].

One wonders if, in defending women's rights to speak, Rev. Baker is responding to his daughter Mary Baker McQuesten's demonstrated matriarchal abilities and intellect—especially as she has accepted the lead in the WFMS (Women's Foreign Missionary Society), and has become very active and very vocal in the Presbyterian Church. For instance, she attended meetings away from home in which she reported on situations like the "Wilkie case" and the "gender wars" among the missionaries, which involved a false accusation of "dancing" against Miss Sinclair by "Rev. Wilkie" [W5172; W4651].

Left: Mary Baker McQuesten (Courtesy Whitehern)

MARY BAKER'S WEDDING TO ISAAC BALDWIN MCQUESTEN: June 18, 1873

*Mary Baker and Isaac McQuesten's wedding photo,
June 18, 1873 (Courtesy Whitehern)*

Mary Baker's wedding to Isaac Baldwin McQuesten was the occasion of much excitement and interest in the Baker and McQuesten households. Mary and Isaac met when Isaac was at the University of Toronto studying law and Mary was at Mrs. Dr. Burns' Ladies' College in Toronto. Isaac appeared to be a good prospect at the time; however, Mary had serious reservations because of

Isaac's excessive use of alcohol, and she broke off the engagement more than once. She extracted a promise that Isaac would give up alcohol, and he promised to do so for at least one year. Nevertheless, Mary finally agreed to the marriage in spite of the obvious presence and use of alcohol, and they decided on the date as June 18, 1873.

A letter from Isaac's friend Robert Hope, in 1869, confirms his reputation as a *mighty mingler* and *drinker of strong drink* [W2275]. *Isaac* also boasts about all the wine he has made *this* year and hopes it will *give some good bellyaches* [2458, November 6, 1875].

Isaac writes to his half-brother, Dr. Calvin Brooks McQuesten, to report that he has: *made 130 or 140 galls of wine this year. Do not know how it will turn out but gave it more care this year than it has ever had before.* In the same letter Isaac acknowledges ordering *and receiving 11B [bushels] of apples.* It is likely these apples that Isaac admits he is using to make hard cider that is like champagne. Then on March 15, 1876, Isaac writes: *The champagne wine is bottled off: 150 bottles & 8 gallons in an iron enamelled cylinder. So, will see what the result will be. Think it will be favourable. But if the cylinder busts, it will be a lively explosion* [W2476].

It was a fairy-tale wedding. As was the custom at the time, seamstresses were called in for several days by Mary and her mother to create a magnificent trousseau. The use of white was not common at that date, since white was considered too extravagant. It uses fabric of a quality and colour which can be worn only once, so most brides opted for a coloured wedding gown, which was more practical for future use.

Fortunately, Mary Baker McQuesten preserved the itemized bill for the trousseau; it was presented to Mary's mother by Sarah Alexander, the seamstress. The complete bill of two pages totals $115.29 and is dated from June 12 to July 7. It is itemized to include all findings, whalebone, ribbon, buttons, sewing silk and linings. The garments made are also listed: Polonaise, Basque, Pannier. This list will be of historical interest when researching the cost of a trousseau, fashions, fabrics and labour in 1873 and comparing them with those of the present day. See the wedding photo, which indicates the voluminous material in Mary's wedding gown. We note also that Mary is seated sideways, which suggests a bustle.

[W3885] TO MRS. REV. THOMAS BAKER from Sarah Alexander [Seamstress]

Jul 11 1873
To:
From:

June 12 [1873]
To making (travelling) overskirt with deep flounce, scalloped pieces and reversed pleating all bound with silk[1]

Polonaise,[2] cape trimmed with pleating	$7.25
Body lining .53, sleeve lining .20, crinoline .30	1.03
Ribbon for cape .75, Dress shields .13	.88
Whalebone, sewing silk	.50

June 13
To making black skirt with deep flounces and ruffles and leaves, Basque[3] apron front, sash trimmed with leaves

all bound with satin	9.25
Body lining .53, crinoline .45, braid .18	1.16
Sleeve lining .25, 3 1/8 yds. Satin 2.87	9.25
Sleeve facing .45, Ribbon .35, Buttons .35	1.15
Whalebone, sewing silk .65. Dress shields .13	.78

June 14
To making one mauve silk skirt with fine finished out ruffles, puffings & puffs in front. Overskirt of

Basque trimmed in pleating piped and turned back	6.75
Body lining .53, skirt lining .75	1.28
Sleeve lining .20, Crinoline .30, Braid .15	.65
4 yds silk 1.25, piped tarleton .75	6.08

Buttons .40, Dress shields .13	.53
Whalebone, sewing silk etc.	.65

June 16
To making dove colour silk shirt with front and sides trimmed with ruffles & double face pleats.

Basque trimmed with folds & turn back tucks	7.75
Body lining .53, skirt lining 1.20	1.85
Sleeve lining .20, Sleeve facing 1.20	1.45
1 1/4 yds corded silk 2.25. Tassels .75	3.56
Ribbon .50, Buttons .28, Braid .18	.96
Crinoline .45, Net for same .17	.62
Dress shields .13, Whalebone, sewing silk .65	.78

June 17
To making one print skirt with four ruffles and two bands above

Polonaise and underbody	3.75
Body lining .25, Buttons .55, Braid .15	.95
Silk Whalebone Thread etc.	.45

July 2
To making one Muslin skirt with nine ruffles in front deep flounce and ruffles in back, Basque and pannier

trimmed with ruffles	4.50
Extra muslin .62, Ribbon for bows .45	1.07
Ribbon for binding .20, Thread .35	.55

July 4
To making one blue silk skirt with 3 ruffles bound in five bands above stitched Empress train trimmed with braid

turn back pieces, Collar and Cuffs	8.00
Body lining .53, Skirt lining .75	1.28
Sleeve lining .20, Crinoline .45, Braid .25	.90

Muslin 1.00. Sleeve facing .45   1.45
4 yds blue silk 2.00. Buttons .80   8.80
Ribbon .30, Buss. shields .13   .43
Whalebone, sewing silk etc.   .75

<u>July 7</u>
To making white muslin skirt, overskirt with Basque
trimmed with pleating   4.25
Extra muslin for skirt and hem   .69
Buttons .30, braid thread etc.   .70

TOTAL $115.29

Received Payment, Toronto July 11, 1873
[signed] Sarah Alexander

THE CHILDREN OF ISAAC AND MARY

Dr. Calvin McQuesten's first son, Dr. Calvin Brooks, had become a doctor and had taken up a practice in New York. He left it to his half-brother, Isaac, to handle all financial matters. Unfortunately, Isaac was an alcoholic and a drug user, was mentally unstable, and mismanaged the estate. He died very suddenly in 1888, as the result of an overdose, and he was bankrupt. Of course, the rumours of suicide were unavoidable, and the stigma had to be endured. Suicide is never mentioned in the letters and Isaac had a large and formal funeral. The doctor who attended Isaac at the last, Dr. Mullins, signed the death certificate that Isaac died of a Coma. (More about Isaac and his tragic story under the heading "Victorian Medicine.")

After Isaac married Mary Baker in 1873 they soon began having children, seven children in twelve years. Many of the extant letters in the Whitehern Archives were written by Mary Baker McQuesten to her children when they were away from home. She stipulated to her children that the letters should be circulated among themselves and then returned back home, where she saved most of the letters. Mary obviously had a strong sense of history, and an even stronger sense of the family's historical importance. Time has shown that this sense was not misdirected.

Six of Isaac and Mary's children lived to adulthood—four girls and two boys (one child, Muriel Fletcher, died at nine months of age). The six children who lived to adulthood are: Mary Baldwin (1874–1964); Calvin (1876–1968); Hilda-Belle (1877–1967); Ruby Baker (1879–1911); Thomas Baker (1882–1948); and Margaret Edna (1886–1936). Each of these children has Victorian stories to be told and some of these accounts have been written up in my earlier book, *Tragedy & Triumph: Ruby & Thomas Baker McQuesten* (2011). Notably, Ruby goes on to become a teacher in Ottawa and sends most of her money home to put Thomas through university to become a lawyer and politician. Thus, he is able finally to restore the family's prestige, if not their wealth.

The two eldest girls, Mary Baldwin and Hilda-Belle, remained single and performed the housemaid duties at Whitehern, as the family could no longer afford to keep servants. Daughter Mary did not receive any proposals, and her mother says of her that she should not consider marriage because "she didn't have the head for it." It is difficult to know what she meant by that. Indeed, none of the six children ever married, and Mary, mother, actively broke up three of her children's engagements, for Hilda-Belle, Tom and Ruby.

Mary Baldwin McQuesten, 1874-1964   Rev. Calvin McQuesten, 1876-1968

Hilda Belle McQuesten, 1877-1967   Ruby Baker McQuesten, 1879-1911

Thomas Baker McQuesten, 1882-1948   Marguerette Edna McQuesten, 1884-1935

THE WEDDING OF REV. THOMAS BAKER'S GRANDDAUGHTER, ALICE BAKER TO EDWARD HARBIN

This story reports on the wedding of Rev. Baker's granddaughter, Alice Baker, who is one of his grandchildren that Rev. Baker has "rescued" from their stepmother, Maria Mudge Baker. The letter is from John Puckridge Baker, Alice's brother. We can see by John's comment that this wedding will serve to place the family on a higher social plane.

[W3429, June 7, 1880] TO REV. THOMAS BAKER, 3 BOLD STREET, HAMILTON, ONTARIO, FROM HIS GRANDSON JOHN PUCKRIDGE BAKER, 312 THAMES STREET, LONDON ONTARIO. [The letter is actually dated May 7th, but the context indicates that June 7th is more likely.]

My dear Grandpa,

I hope that you are not annoyed at me for the unbusiness like manner in which I have treated your letter of the 1st inst. containing the remittance of [$35.00?], and also for the length of time you have been waiting an answer to yours of the [19th?] of May. In explanation, I will confirm what you have no doubt concluded viz. that for a considerable time both before and after the wedding we had from two to [four?] guests constantly with us, added to which, for several days previous to the wedding we had [three?] and four dressmakers in the house all the time, to say nothing about the [buying?], cooking, planing [sic] &c., &c., which invariably attend such occasions.

I must however be careful to ask you, not to judge as to the [grandeur?] of the preparations by the [patter?] which we made over them. Alice, I think it may have been for the purpose of keeping Miss Harbin and others in the dark, had made no previous preparations whatever, our house was small, the weather unbearably hot, and our experience in such preparations very limited; so, you can easy imagine that we did not accomplish nearly what might have been expected from the amount of trouble and expense that was gone to. However, I am happy to be able to tell you that not one of our arrangements ended incomplete, *and though most of them [much?] exceeded our calculations we have the benefit of the experience for our [extra?] trouble and expense. It may be pertinent here to remark that Minnie says, if she were going to get married we could have everything just as nice as Alice did, without going to more than one half of the trouble or expense; which (as I do not think it in the least likely that poor Min. will ever take a fancy to a "Mr. Harbin") I consider a very happy conclusion.*

In your letter to Minnie you expressed something of a desire to hear about the wedding, and a hope that everything passed off pleasantly, I can assure you that it did, and that in consideration of the kind of match which Alice was making, and the position in life in which it was going to place her, we spared nothing that was within our power to secure to see that it did pass off both pleasantly and well. Owing to our having the acquaintance of but very few gentlemen suitable to invite, and as it was wished that the public should not anticipate the event, we concluded to extend invitations only among our own connection. They were married at half past three, in St. Paul's Cathedral by the Rev. Canon [Sims?]. Attending them at the altar, were Minnie, and my Sister-in-law Miss Gullen, for Brides-maids; each with their hair in ringlets, each dressed in white, one trimmed with cardinal and the other with pale blue and each carrying a miniature boquett [sic]. The Ladies were dressed in white tarlatan, the Bride's trimmed with white Satin, Minnie's with Cardinal, and Miss Gullen's with pale blue. The Gentlemen with frock coats, black pants, and white vests. Dr. Balmer for Groomsman, Myself to give away the Bride, and last but not in every sense least, came Alfred, with one of Mrs. Puckridge's little girls about the same size, each with large black eyes.

Aunt Jane and Lottie went to see them married. Willie who did not arrive in time to be provided for here had nothing fit to wear for the occasion. But I think that he made up at the breakfast and enjoyed himself as well as any of us.

----- I am called to go out and will have to leave off in the middle of my letter without having touched upon the most important [points?] but will be home on [Wednesday?] and will then send you the remainder with kindest love [?] to you all in which Minnie joins me,

I remain your affect. G-son [grandson]
John P. Baker

DR. CALVIN MCQUESTEN, THE INDUSTRIAL TYCOON (1801–1885)

Dr. Calvin McQuesten came from the United States and built the first foundry in Hamilton, Ontario, in 1835. It was at James and Merrick Streets. As a result, in time, Hamilton became known as "The Birmingham of Canada." The first foundry suffered a fire in 1855. The second foundry was built at the foot of Wellington Street in 1870.

Dr. Calvin McQuesten retired in 1857 and eventually sold to his nephews, the Sawyers. The company eventually became the Sawyer-Massey Co.

There are many letters from Dr. Calvin McQuesten to his cousin John Fisher at the foundry, and from Fisher at the foundry back to Calvin during difficult family and labour problems and political troubles. See also: [W-MCP4-6.171, Feb. 20, 1838; W-MCP4-6.201; W-MCP4-6.236; W-MCP4-6.189; W-MCP4-6.183; W-MCP4-6.169; W-MCP4-6.194; W-MCP4-6.184]. For more on John Fisher, see [W-MCP5-6.24.0].

The letter below opens: ***We are in the beginning of a civil war***, which is a reference to the 1837 Rebellion of Upper Canada. We can see by the dates of the births and deaths of Dr. Calvin McQuesten's children that he was absent from Hamilton and his foundry, and that he was with his wife at Brockport, N.Y. while she required medical attention during the births of their first two sons: Calvin Jr. August 15–25, 1834; and Calvin Brooks 1837–1912.

[W-MCP4-6.193], December 7, 1837 TO DR. CALVIN AND MARGARETTE MCQUESTEN BROCKPORT, MONROE COUNTY, NEW YORK U.S.A., FROM THEIR COUSINS JOHN AND CATHERINE FISHER, HAMILTON, UPPER CANADA

Dear Cousin,

We are in the beginning of a civil war *[emphasis added]. We shall probably deeply regret that we came to this province—& this morning sent the Children to Warsaw to Mother—Catherine remains* at present—We have no mail from the east side of the Lake—Quebec Montreal Toronto &co they have robbed it once and now there is no one sent. —This was done by McKenzie on the night of the 6th—It is now reported that not a letter which has the least appearance of any importance is permitted to pass without being opened.

Our business is at an end—in a few days I shall stop work entirely unless things change of which there is no prospect. You will want to know something of our affairs probably more than I can write. I may be at Brockport in some days. I can do nothing more than put our accounts into notes and make them as secure as I can. —No one thinks of paying an account no more than if he had a receipt in full. I know not what will be the result—I would leave the place were it not the fear of losing our furnace by fire and having the property destroyed. In relation to Janes, he had sold all but 3 of the machines and I suppose his notes are as good as any and of the amount he expects. Mr. Backus will be rather concerned about his debt—We have a Cavalry force under arms day and night to guard us.

Parker—he lays in irons and there is the determination to execute him. It requires more strength of nerve than I possess to speak of the transaction without giving utterance to language which might be thought very [subversive? suspicious?] He had been my best friend— Those direct from Toronto state that there was a hot engagement last night in which 30 riflemen were killed and 40 made prisoners. All is consternation.

Davis & Ford [engaged?] to be here by today and make some arrangement by which I should obtain some money. They have not yet written should they come—will start to Montreal unless some remain of our friends who are fleeing should present a favourable offer [?] to send.—The Country is ruined for years and ages. There is not a $100 or 50 dollars to be received in all Hamilton. There is no credit for any thing with but few exceptions—each man is suspicious of his neighbour—.

John Fisher

[Page continues with a note from Catherine Blanchard (Fisher) to Margarette Lerned McQuesten.]

Dear Cousin Margaret, these are troublesome times. Poor Mr.

Parker lies in prison and his family are overwhelmed in sorrow. I write with an aching head and heart. My little children are on the road to Warsaw and you must know that I shall not spend many happy hours untill [sic]I get news of their safe arrival at Warsaw. We live under very unpleasant circumstances in constant fear that our lives and property are in danger. I cannot consent to leave without Mr. Fisher and he is determined to stay untill he is obliged to flee for his life. My poor little children riding over these bad roads in an open carriage my heart almost breaks at the thought. Do write to us as soon as you receive this. How is your health and your little one?

In haste affectionately yours, Catherine Fisher

[Letter continues in John Fisher's hand:]

It is very doubtful when you receive this. There is no mail but by boat to Toronto via Queenston, Lewiston & on. When we will start no one knows—the direct mail is cut off, some expect Martial Law in a few days. John Fisher

A point of clarification: It should be noted that many people have come to speculate that Dr. Calvin McQuesten did not own the foundry and that his cousin Fisher owned it. This is because of the many letters from Fisher at the foundry to Dr. McQuesten at Brockport, New York. The letter from Fisher to Dr. McQuesten, dated December 7, 1837 is a good example here. Dr. Calvin McQuesten's first wife, Margarette Lerned, had three sons: Calvin Jr. (August 15–25, 1834); Calvin Brooks (1837–1912); and James Barker (July 10–29, 1841), who came later while they were living in Hamilton. Margarette Lerned died three days after the birth of James Barker, and the child died nineteen days after the birth; both died in Hamilton, Ontario. However, Calvin Brooks McQuesten, born in 1837, survived. He eventually became a doctor and practised in New York.

In 1839 Dr. Calvin McQuesten and his wife, Margaret Barker Lerned McQuesten, made a permanent move to Hamilton, and then he could participate fully in the running of his foundry.

After the tragedy of losing his first wife, Dr. Calvin married Estimate Esther Ruth Baldwin on September 11, 1844. She had two children: Isaac Baldwin McQuesten (1847–1888) and David McQuesten (1851–1854). Estimate died in April 1851. Her son David survived his birth but died as the result of a stove fire at Whitehern (then "Willowbank") on December 8, 1854.

Whitehern Historic House and Garden, c.1940
(Courtesy Whitehern)

ELIZABETH FULLER MCQUESTEN, "THE WICKED STEPMOTHER"

In 1852/3, Dr. Calvin McQuesten moved with his three sons into Whitehern (then called Willowbank). He felt that he needed to seek a new mother for his three sons. In 1853 he married Elizabeth Fuller and she moved into Whitehern to become "The Wicked Stepmother" of the story. She earned that epithet because she demonstrated that she did not like children, sent them away to school, loved to spend money, and was very vain. The children soon came to call her "the O.L." for "Old Lady."

Elizabeth Fuller McQuesten
(Courtesy Whitehern)

Dr. Calvin McQuesten was a very astute businessman and he earned a fortune, but he made two very serious mistakes in his life. His **first** serious mistake occurred in marrying Elizabeth Fuller in 1853 and bringing her into the house. There are many letters in the archive of the family problems between Elizabeth Fuller and Dr. McQuesten and his two sons.

The following excerpt of a letter that she wrote home to Willowbank demonstrates her capacity for shopping and spending. However, it is acknowledged that many of the fine furnishings at Whitehern today are likely due to her extravagances.

[W1213, October 17, 1855] TO DR. CALVIN MCQUESTEN, HAMILTON, ONTARIO, CANADA, FROM HIS WIFE ELIZABETH FULLER MCQUESTEN, BOSTON, MASSACHUSETTS.

My dear, very dear Husband,

Everything has been as pleasant as possible since I left home and I did hope to see you at home the last of this week, but it would be a pity not to spend a little more money, since I came so rich; so, I must spend a few days here in order to lighten my purse ... The screen is to be packed and sent as freight today. I hope it will not arrive before I do since I fear that no glance of admiration would fall on me till that was out of sight. I hope it will go safe. I have seen a picture that would answer, Price $350.00! ...

Good morning My dear. Peace be with you. Lizzie

Note that the exclamation mark at the end of Elizabeth's letter is her own.

Dr. Calvin McQuesten's **second** serious mistake occurred when he appointed his son Isaac Baldwin McQuesten as his financial surrogate, to administer his estate.

Dr. Calvin McQuesten soon learned that he could not trust his new wife, Elizabeth. She argued with her husband frequently—and with his son, Isaac. Isaac reported these sessions to his half-brother, Dr. Calvin Brooks in New York, and they both agreed to thwart Elizabeth Fuller McQuesten wherever possible, with their father's legal approval. They drew up a new and secret will which their father approved and signed.

When Dr. Calvin McQuesten died on October 20, 1885 Elizabeth was dispatched to the United States, and her annuity was paid to her by her stepson, Dr. Calvin Brooks McQuesten. The annuity came from some real estate that Dr. Calvin Brooks received in the settlement of his father's estate, the Alexandria Arcade. Elizabeth was very angry but could do nothing since the legal work had been done by Isaac's partner, James Chisholm.

HILDA-BELLE'S THWARTED ROMANCE

*Kenelm Trigge (above)
and
Hilda Belle McQuesten
(right)
(courtesy Whitehern)*

Mary wrote to her son Calvin to express her concern about Hilda's engagement:

[W4635, August 10, 1902, MARY BAKER MCQUESTEN, WHITEHERN, TO HER SON, CALVIN MCQUESTEN IN MONTREAL]
Dear Calvin:
Ken [Trigge] was just here and his visit was the occasion of most trying experience for all concerned. Of course, I had to have a very plain talk with him and when I spoke to him of his not being an abstainer, he was very frank and open, but simply said that for him to be an abstainer meant that he must throw up his position and then I discovered that it was all far worse than I imagined. It is his business to be most

agreeable to the firm's customers and to this end Mr. Beardmore gives him and instructs him to go to any expense in treating, asking men to lunch or dinner and when he does so of course he must drink or smoke with them. Well, of course, I said it was far worse than I had any idea, that I always heard a traveller's life was one of great temptation but I thought it meant that others would ask him to drink but, in this case, he was asking others, in fact was making his living by tempting men to do wrong. What an awful position! So, I said I could never consent.

On explaining the state of affairs to H.[Hilda] she agreed with me, but it was a most distressing time and really made us ill. Ken felt so terribly, particularly as he said, there was nothing else he could do and all business is carried on in this way. But Hilda I must say was wonderfully brave and conscientious and though she had quite determined to take him, she withstood him and said no, she would not marry a man whose living was made in such a way. He himself said, that no one had ever put it before him as we had, that he was given liquor at home from when he was twelve years old and never knew it was any harm. But now, he said, he saw, that he was committing a sin every day of his life. But where to find another situation is the difficulty. It does seem a most iniquitous thing, this treating system. Sincerely, M.B. McQuesten

At this time Hilda was twenty-five years of age. Kenelm Trigge was the son of Captain Trigge and Mrs. Trigge of "Auchmar," a large estate on the Hamilton mountain. Captain Trigge was a member of the Plymouth Brethren, and Kenelm's prospects were good. We can speculate on what would have been the outcome if Hilda and Ken had married and if Hilda had become the chatelaine of "Auchmar." They might have had children and "Auchmar" might have been preserved, whereas it is in ruin today (although with some hope of recovery).

In 1905 a letter from one of Calvin's newspaper friends (incomplete and unsigned) states that Ken *is even less of an abstainer than he was when we dwelt on Sherbrooke* [W7553]. The McQuestens' experience with Isaac's alcoholism, which contributed to his death, had created a very strong temperance commitment in the household.

Significantly, the temperance referendum was being hotly debated in the city in 1902 and the McQuestens were actively campaigning against alcohol; the vote was to be held in December 1902. As Mary notes, Hilda would have accepted Ken but Mary prevailed upon her until she rejected him, and so Hilda remained a spinster for the rest of her life. She died in 1977 at the age of 90 and is buried in the family plot in the Hamilton Cemetery.

THOMAS BAKER MCQUESTEN'S THWARTED ROMANCE

The first mention of Isabel Elliot occurs when Mary (mother) is visiting Toronto for Tom's law school convocation on June 1, 1907. She states that: *Grey came in escorting Miss Isabel Elliot.* Then at the end of the letter, Mary writes: *We have also heard from Mrs. Culhain that our Tom is engaged and that the whole thing is settled, to whom is not mentioned.* [W5868]

Mary does not get a chance to speak with Tom at that graduation, but she soon learns that Tom is engaged to a Miss Isabel Elliot. John Best, historian, has done some further research which shows that Miss Isabel Elliot was a fellow-student at U of T with Tom, and she was in the graduating class in 1905. Tom went on to graduate in law in 1907. Isabel's photo appears in the 1905 U of T graduation catalogue along with the notation:

A countenance in which did meet, Sweet records, promises so sweet. Although Born in Brampton, Isabel Elliot graduated from the Parkdale Collegiate and entered the English and History Courses of '05. One of the sweetest and most charming of the many charming girls in the year, her unfailing sympathy and evenness of disposition have made her deservedly popular, as may be seen from the fact that she has held office in the Class Executive, the Women's Lit., and the Women's Athletic Association. Isabel will have the best wishes in whatever career she elects to follow.

Mary objected to the engagement and Miss Elliot attempted to win her favour by arranging to have Mary's miniature painted by a Miss Ramsay. However, Mary found fault at each stage of the painting and the retouching. The romance continued in secret for a time and Miss Elliot wrote letters to Tom at Whitehern *in a masculine hand* from October 1906 to April 1907. In one letter Isabel states: *Love me love my dog,* and we have a photo:

Miss Isabel Elliot and dog (Courtesy Whitehern)

It is not known how long the relationship continued or when it was terminated. However, Tom never married.

1888, Tom at age 6 in long pants. [P.S. Boys wore dresses until they could manage a button fly. Zippers were not invented until the early 1900s.] (Courtesy Whitehern)

1905, Tom graduation, U. of T. (Courtesy Whitehern)

[REV.] CALVIN MCQUESTEN: DISABLED LEFT HAND, MENTAL FRAGILITY AND FAITH HEALING

Above: Calvin as a young boy (left); Rev. Calvin's graduation/ ordination, 1909 (Both Courtesy Whitehern)

Rev. Calvin McQuesten (1875–1968), the eldest son of Isaac and Mary, was disabled in his left hand and on his left side. This can be seen in the family photo with mother Mary McQuesten, and in the photos of Calvin with his canoe, and with Jack Miner. However, he went on to work his way through school, and to graduate from university. His ordination as a Presbyterian minister took place at the age of thirty-three, but in 1925 he voted in referendum to change and to become a United Church minister, much to his family's disgust.

However, his reasons were valid: all of the Presbyterian churches were voting either to remain Presbyterian or to switch to the newly formed United Church. The McQuestens were steadfastly voting to remain Presbyterian but Calvin was campaigning for the

United Church. This caused great dissension in the family. Calvin remembered that when he was an itinerant minister out west, he had to travel on horseback to three different churches on a Sunday. He believed that having one United Church would solve problems for himself and for many other ministers in the west. The MacNab Street Presbyterian Church voted to remain Presbyterian but many of the other Presbyterian Churches voted to join the new United Church.

Rev. Calvin McQuesten was a deeply religious person and in 1896 he became a convert to the "Zion" Divine Healing Mission in Chicago. He had fallen under the influence of Rev. John Alexander Dowie and his "Zion" Divine Healing Mission. Calvin joined the Dowieites for healing in 1896 after he suffered an emotional collapse brought on by the stress of examinations after his first year at University of Toronto. He failed Mathematics and English and was forced to transfer from Honours Classics to a Pass program (W-MCP1-3b.068). The Dowie influence had a profound and long-lasting effect on Calvin and his diary entry of 1933 refers to his *rebirth in 1896* (W-MCP1-3b.016).

In July 25, 1896, Calvin writes to his mother to ask her for the funds to remain with the Dowieites at the Zion Divine Healing Mission; and he also invites his mother to come to Chicago to become part of the Dowieites. Mother was not pleased and replied to Calvin:

[W-MCP1-3B.016, July 25, 1896] TO [REV.] CALVIN MCQUESTEN, (in care of) "ZION" DIVINE HEALING MISSION, CORNER MICHIGAN AVE. AND 12TH **ST. CHICAGO, ILLINOIS; FROM HIS MOTHER, MARY BAKER MCQUESTEN, WHITEHERN, HAMILTON**

My dear Calvin,

You must indeed have got into the clouds when you proposed my starting off to Chicago. You seem to have quite forgotten that I had to borrow the money that took you and that money was what I always set aside for my taxes. Nothing could have induced me to break in upon that, but the almost certainty that you would be able to earn the money that would replace it. And I do not wish to discourage you but you must come home well before I would think of going. I am regaining my strength very slowly indeed, but as the weather is cooler I hope to get along faster. I am much exercised as to what you can do by next Monday, if you are not yet cured. If you think you had better stay longer you must let me know and I will see what I can do. It tries me so to write and makes me so nervous that I can›t write any more. May God help you and strengthen your faith. Your loving Mother, M.B. McQuesten[1]

Calvin suffered emotional collapse whenever under stress, which occurred when taking examinations. Before entering the ministry, he attempted several careers, including journalism. At the *Montreal Herald* he wrote a news column, "The Tatler," and at Copp Clark he wrote several columns, among them a women's column under the pseudonym "Nina Vivian," which was the name of a female impersonator. These columns and their contents are on the Whitehern website.

For a time, Calvin was a homesteader in Saskatchewan. He built a "shack" on his homestead, and had a crop planted, but the

---

1. John Alexander Dowie was born in Scotland in 1847 and came to the United States in 1888 by way of Australia. He formed one of the most successful faith healing ministries in the United States. He declared that he was Elijah the Restorer and wore High-Priestly robes. In 1896 his ministry headquarters was a seven-storey building on a city block in Chicago, and by 1901 he owned 6,000 acres of land near Chicago where he built his "Zion City." He and his wife fell into financial ruin when they began to indulge in secular activities, such as personal mansion building and Paris vacations. He was deposed in 1906 and died almost bankrupt in 1907. Dowie's work has become of interest to the healing revivalists and millenialists of the present day and his sermons were published in 1996 (CBD 437; *The Biographical Dictionary* [September 9, 1998]: Online, October 4, 1998).

In 1901 Dowie spoke to a crowd of 10,000 and devoted much of his time to abusing the press and concluded that he might start a daily paper in Chicago (*The Evening News*, Toronto, January 23, 1901). An article in *The Montreal Herald* of December 6, 1902 carried the title, "John Alexander Dowie, Merchant Prince of Faith Healing, makes $15,000,000 in Ten Years." A Montreal branch of the Dowieites was formed, and on June 10, 1903 another *Herald* article noted the rather peculiar state of affairs, in which the Queen St. Baptist Colored Church was attempting to raise the funds to get rid of the Dowieites with whom they were sharing the church. It is not known if Calvin attended this church in Montreal; however, he may have written these articles as he was a journalist with each paper at the time of publication.

crop was destroyed by hail in 1910 and he was forced to give up [W-MCP6-1.410, 1910/9/13]. He was also an itinerant preacher in Alberta and Saskatchewan. Calvin wrote a book, *The King of Fighting Men*, but it was never published. It too is on the Whitehern website [Box 04-028 & 033]. Between 1920 and 1950 he was the much-loved United Church chaplain of the Hamilton Mountain Sanatorium.

Calvin had a real fondness for the French-Canadian people and spent much time at Gaspe. He gave readings of the Drummond poems in an authentic French-Canadian patois. He also kept a diary, which appears on the website in five parts, much of which is devotional, but he also discloses family matters [Box15-001a; Box 15-001b; Box 15-001c, 1859; Box 14-001, 1918; Box 14-064, 1923, selections].

Calvin had a many-varied career, although he never earned enough money to keep himself. Unfortunately, he was never able to earn a steady income until he became the chaplain of the tuberculosis sanatorium in 1920. Even that was a semi-volunteer position and did not pay a large salary. Before 1920 Calvin was rarely at home, so his mother was frequently writing to him, and there are many letters to Calvin on the site, as well as his diary. Calvin provides much richness to the website.

Calvin with Jack Miner; note Calvin's disabled left hand (Courtesy Whitehern)

Portage at Cootes Paradise, Hamilton. Note Calvin's limp left hand; he required assistance whenever he went out with his canoe, which was often (Courtesy Whitehern).

Photo noted as Camille (possibly) (Courtesy Whitehern).

ADDRESS BY REV. CALVIN MCQUESTEN TO THE HAMILTON PARKS BOARD

Calvin decided that Whitehern should be deeded to the City of Hamilton after his and his sisters' deaths. Following is the address that he delivered at the regular meeting of the Hamilton Parks Board on Monday, November 3, 1959. When Dr. Connell, chairman of the Parks Board, had conveyed to the McQuesten family the thanks of the Board and the people of Hamilton, Rev Calvin McQuesten rose and replied:

[BOX 08-140, November 3, 1959]

Mr. Chairman, gentlemen; this is definitely a case where it is more blessed to give than to receive. The completion of this transaction has brought me more pleasure and satisfaction than anything that has happened to me since, more than sixty-two years ago, I first began to realize the greatness of God's love for me and to recognize that the greatest fact in life for me is the fact that God is my Father and that He loves me more than any human father ever loved a son.

There are two reasons for this happiness and satisfaction which I feel tonight. The first, and lesser reason is the joy of knowing that this house, of which Professor Eric Arthur says that he knows of no house in Canada so worthy of preservation, will not fall into the hands of the wreckers; and the many interesting and beautiful things in it be scattered to the four winds.

The second and deeper reason for my satisfaction and happiness is that in this transaction I am able to make reparation for a great wrong committed by my family and many other families in a similar position. You will often hear old people of a certain class lament the passing of an age of gracious living as exemplified in such a home as Whitehern. I do not. And I say so with the greatest intensity of emphasis of which I am capable.

For in the very next block to the north-west of Whitehern was 'Bread-ticket Row'—the meanest slum in Hamilton. 'Bread-ticket Row' was so called because the man who built it, and lived in the large stone house north of it on Main Street, recently occupied by the One-Two Club, used to collect the rent in person, and when a tenant was unable to pay all his rent in cash, and he saw any bread-tickets lying around, he would pick them up and put them in his pocket. When he built 'Bread-ticket Row,' even though land must have been cheap in those days, he chose what was probably the narrowest block in Hamilton—so narrow that the back yard of each was smaller than the smallest room in Whitehern except the hall bedroom and the bathrooms, so small that there was no room for anything but the clothes-lines, with which many of the tenants' wives eked out a meagre living. Whitehern, with its spacious and lovely lawns and gardens, occupied just an even acre. The twelve houses of 'Bread-ticket Row' were all crammed into about a quarter of that space.

Gentlemen, I am glad that instead of such shameful inequality between the 'gracious living' of homes like Whitehern and the wretched squalor of slums like 'Bread-ticket Row' we may drive or walk today through miles of streets of lovely little homes of equal size and an incredible variety of beautiful designs, each owned by the family living in it.

And I hope that many of the people who in earlier years knew the bitterness of the squalor of such slums and the children who were born in them may enjoy, whenever they please, the beautiful rooms of Whitehern and eat their lunches in its pleasant garden.

Calvin had enlisted the help of Professor Eric Arthur from the School of Architecture at the University of Toronto in order to help convince Mary and Hilda to donate the house, Whitehern, to the city of Hamilton after their deaths. At the time this particular letter was written, the sisters were determined to bequeath the house to the church. Mary, Calvin and Hilda's ages were (respectively) 84, 82 and 81, but they all lived into their 90s. Neither they nor any of their siblings had any descendants to whom the property could be bequeathed.

Since Rev. Calvin outlived his sisters, he spent some time in his final years organizing all the letters and artifacts stored at Whitehern, for which Hamilton and history can be grateful. For the documents relating to Calvin's "scheme" to convince his sisters to bequeath Whitehern to the Hamilton Parks Board, see the following in chronological order: [Box 04-111, 1958/09/29; W8697a, 1958/10/06; W8701a, 1958/10/06; W8273, 1958/11/06; Box 04-012, 1958/11/06; Box 04-113, 1958/11/07; Box 05-002, 1959/02/01; Box 09-233, 1959/11/04; Box 14-090, 1960/06/18; Box 04-113a, 1971/05/04].

Rev. Calvin McQuesten with nurse at the tuberculosis sanatorium "The San" in Hamilton (Courtesy Whitehern).

WORLD WAR ONE, 1914 TO 1918

Thomas McQuesten had wanted to enlist in WWI, but his mother argued vociferously against it. Mary Baker McQuesten's violent opposition to the war is coloured by the fact that Tom wanted to enlist, just as his friend Norman Leslie and his law partner, Chisholm, and many others, had done. Tom and his mother had great rows over this, and it was a long-protracted family crisis; but in the end Mary Baker McQuesten, the Victorian Matriarch, won out and Tom did not enlist. Even his brother Calvin tried to intercede on his behalf but his mother was adamant. Calvin wrote brief prayers in his diary: *that Tom may go ... that mother may tell him so.* Mary stated, repeatedly: *We do not like the way men do things.* She lamented: *O dear Yes! The war is so terrible and all these young Canadians cut off in the prime of life and their mothers left to mourn them all their days. I feel so distressed, because I am afraid until there is a recognition of sin and repentance as God requires of His ancient people, there will be no help from Him* [W6828]. *The war news seems terrible just now, it hangs over one, and we feel as if we didn't know what would happen next. It seems so fearful to think of the awful slaughter, thousands of men handed over to death. Such fine fellows too! It makes one ill to think of it, and no one can stop it, we are just helpless* [W6820].

The widowed Mary Baker McQuesten feared losing her favourite son Tom and his salary, and his potential to restore the family. Tom's was the only salary for the family since his sister Ruby had died in 1911, and he was the family's only hope for the future. They had made many sacrifices for his education, especially Ruby, who had worked as a teacher just long enough to pay his way through university in law. In spite of many arguments, Mary managed to keep Tom at home. However, receipts found in the Whitehern Archives indicate that, despite her opposition to the war, Mary donated money to the war effort.

Norman Victor Leslie and Thomas Baker McQuesten at a rugby match, second row left and centre (Courtesy Whitehern).

DR. NORMAN VICTOR LESLIE WRITES FROM THE TRENCHES IN WORLD WAR ONE:
WHAT WAR REALLY MEANS I KNOW NOW

Dr. Norman V. Leslie (1883–1947) was a good friend of the McQuesten family of Whitehern. During the war, he sent many letters home to Thomas Baker McQuesten about his service in the trenches in France, which he describes graphically. The complete set of letters is preserved in the Whitehern Archives. The first, which is not copied here, is written on the ship going over to England, when Dr. Leslie is in a buoyant mood. Of the many letters to Tom, the following three are those that describe conditions as experienced by an active surgeon at the front. The three letters appear here in their entirety since they best convey Dr. Leslie's experiences, his personality, and his relationship with Tom McQuesten.

[W-MCP6-1.458; October 17, 1915] FROM DR. NORMAN V. LESLIE; #2 CANADIAN GENERAL HOSPITAL [FRANCE] TO THOMAS B. MCQUESTEN, WHITEHERN, HAMILTON

Cher T.B. [Thomas Baker McQuesten]

You cast dust on my name. I do write and have answered every letter of yours. So, Gordon Southam is a Major. Good. He will make good no doubt, but one can't help thinking of the many captains and lieutenants out since the first, who one would imagine would be given the chance of promotion. This business is one of favor and interest from top to bottom thru' and thru' [?] a pull; such is the [?] Are we ever going to get a chance to sink somebody? You perhaps notice that Hugh's son is a Brigadier General. Great! From Captain to Major (I am not sure which), to Brigadier. Shades of Napoleon, and all in a year.

After the last big affair, we were certainly busy getting very serious cases and lashings of them. Poor devils. Such hellish injuries, bones smashed to splinters, great chunks of flesh and muscle torn away, and on top of that pus running from them: nearly all, and very frequently gas-gangrene and infections which develops with great rapidity and eats up and destroys good healthy tissue. The buglers of the camp were busy calling the last post for a time. This is the hideous part. The beautiful part is the way the Tommy takes his wounds—quite silent in pain and facing a maimed future with cheery fortitude. They are wonders. The stories they write about the soldier are very true. He is working hard.

They like the Canadians very much, nurses and doctors. Their superiors, many of them do not (we reciprocate) we are a rather dreadful lot and cause them a great deal of worry about us and our morals. We really are not so dreadful, but some of them are so smug and so virtuous, and really cannot mind their own affairs. But I am [?]—so go buy yourself a drink with this. Write! Who am I going to [?]

Yours, Norman Leslie.

[W-MCP6-1.46; August 16, 1916] FROM DR. NORMAN V. LESLIE, FRANCE TO THOMAS B. MCQUESTEN, WHITEHERN, HAMILTON, ONTARIO

My Dear Tom, Your letter to hand. I had not gotten your letter or tobacco or the tabac itself but thank you just the same. Well old dear, this is somewhat different from the base hospital. Of course, the work in the hospital is far better every way. Here the opportunities for medical work are necessarily limited. You look at a man and send him out. But on the other hand, are lots of excitements etc. The life at least so far is not monotonous; one sees all sorts of grim things and hears the most unconscionable rackets. The roar and bark of our guns is most annoying, and always jolts one considerably. It is so sudden and penetrating. The sound of the enemy shells is even more disconcerting as they have a very tangible bite to their bark to them.

As for adventures: Well! A medical officer's life is not a patch on the soldier's who has to be in the trenches all the time but even tho' one has his narrow escapes. I have had two or three narrow ones, that is comparatively narrow where the luck broke my way, but they are really not worth recounting for so many others have had so many really narrow brushes and they say nothing of it. All the same the life is very wearing and men very soon show the strain tho' they stay with it just the same.

Am very glad George [Norman Leslie's brother] *has done so well, and in a way am sorry to see him start for he is likely to get it. That is the usual outcome. Still that is what he has gone in for. He will get over I think.*

[Baines?] father has certainly got the local touch down cold. His view and little bits of scenery are easily seen all over the place. He knows this life all right. It is a scene of utter desolation all right, wrecked buildings, dug outs stuck everywhere and nothing seen but soldiers. Grass and weeds grow everywhere. In the trenches you see blue cornflowers and red poppies sprouting up from the bags, a pretty sight in its way.

Then the rats. Their name is legion. You see grass stirring and a slinking form sneak along in the day. Then at night they become very bold. There are several devils that come into my abode every night. There is a sort of window. You cast your eye at this, and there are two or three peering at you, and when it is quiet they slip into the room. I hate them but have been able to kill none yet. Occasionally you see a wild cat that has remained true to its name, but these cats don't seem able to handle the [question?]. They are very thin poor things. Truly this is a strange place, and it is going to be a great problem after the war. There is such ruin and there will be so many dead to dispose of. They are everywhere.

Well old top write again,
Yours,
Norman Leslie

[W-MCP6-1.462; October 15, 1916] FROM DR. NORMAN LESLIE, [FRANCE] TO THOMAS B. MCQUESTEN, WHITEHERN, HAMILTON, ONTARIO

My Dear Tom, yours received and glad as always was I to hear from you. I have got as I remember one package—Bull Durham tobacco from you, but I have received one package not named, of pipe tobacco, and I have received two packages from Miss McMeekin's florist & Drewery's Drug Store. These as I infer are her own private gift to me (warn squalls) and I am taking them as such. So, one of your packages has probably gone astray. But please have your card put in so you get the benefit of my prayers, not as unknown, so all will then be right and proper as should be.

As you say, I should get leave to Canada, and believe me I am going to have a try. As for resigning, I think I will stick it out though when I have spent six months or more up, I think I will have a try for England. I never have been there and should have little trouble in getting it as I have spent about two years in France. Still I don't know but what I like France and probably will be dead keen on getting back. My life at the Front I like. True there are certain times when one wishes he hadn't but those times are not frequent, and one has to take the thick with the thin, and at that my position is so much better than the first lines, that I really by comparison am quite safe. The recent fighting in which the Canadians have figured and that well has been severe but the losses compared with what was gained are slight.

I have gained a great respect for the Germans as a dugout builder. These dugouts are up to 30 feet deep, sloping shafts generally two, sunk into the chalk, and at its bottom generally a passage with small rooms cut out. These stairs at one time were away from the direction of fire, but as the dugouts changed hands, what were the back doors, naturally became the front doors, and as Fritz had the range of these dugouts the porch became a sorting place. Some casualties resulted from this, but down below, one was safe tho' alarmed for to have a shell hit above you or near you caused a disturbance which did not make for comfort. The dugouts themselves, some of the ones taken over were terribly dirty equipment British and German and smell very badly from more horrible causes. The Germans had made bunks and on these were pillowcases. These often were blood soaked and horrible. Some did not have the dead cleared out till our own men did it. Some of the sights on the road and trenches recently taken were horrible. Seared themselves into my brain. I know dead in all sorts of attitudes and conditions. At that time, it was impossible to clear them. We had enough to do with the living and it is not right to risk the living for the dead. But we clean up quickly and are decent burying as soon as possible so by now all will be gone and identified.

What war really means I know now [emphasis added]. *The sights, sounds and conditions are terrible; but shining through it all, the manly virtues; courage, steadfastness and self sacrifice. The officers and men hold and advance through hell and after it all as willingly risk themselves again to help the wounded. And the wounded themselves take their often-heavy burden and bleak future with a bright courage* *that often is heart breaking. They are truly a fine lot. As for souvenirs, there are lashings of them and our men came out with a great many odds and ends. I could have got heaps but ongoing in and out; one if he is wise and of a prudent nature, travels as light as possible. There are sounds in the air which are the best physical stimulants I know of. One does not stand on the order of going, but goes. I am becoming agile and can hurl myself on my face with true circus like dispatch and neatness, and I have got much practice at that. So, the less equipment one carries I find the better. I believe in burrowing into the breast of Mother Nature. So, few souvenirs for me but a whole skin.*

But to go back to dugouts. Fritz wrought well but he left his card on many. After my first tour I itched in the wrists thru' the chest tummy and knees. Lord it was awful. I tore myself to pieces. The itch is back. I became almost naked and unashamed. I scratched in public and before rank. Ralph [?] came into my dressing station when his lot took over, and even in the face of [Christ?] and the Cloth did I undo myself and scrape, scrape. The Duke of Argyll was a truly great man and to be blessed. [The Duke of Argyll erected posts on his estate upon which the animals could rub and scratch themselves]. But the itch is now gone, praise be to perseverance and chirurgical skill and certain cunning unguents. Never did I know a better patient.

If you want to send me some tobacco as you hinted, send me some [Brahadhis?] Guards Mixture. Drewery knows the kind. A man here, like the sick, takes fancies principally because he pictures the place and the friends it comes from. I get lots of Colton here, the best, but like great desires for the kinds I knew. I can picture the places at home; not homesick now, but a sort of dream land where I was happy and did not know it. I am happy enough here all right, but it is different.

I guess old lad you are having a hard time of it running the whole ranch by yourself, but as you have a fair (not physically) head on yourself, you will do it properly I know. Am glad to hear Logie is doing well. He is a clever man. I heard from George. He sent me a pipe on my birthday, the first knowledge I got of him, and a pleasant one. He is doing well I think, and I am most glad. The old story about blood being thicker is most true I find, and I watch his progress with anxiety. He is showing his good qualities and a great deal of feeling and good sense, which makes him a fine fellow.

But I find I have written a prodigious long letter and most

disjointed one I fear, and as the candle is down and as alas I now am like the early lark I will say goodnight.
Your old friend,
Norman Leslie
P.S. Please remember me to your mother and sisters.

Dr. Norman Leslie's letters indicate the bravery and the stoicism that he and the Canadian soldiers displayed during the First World War. However, there is an indication in the Whitehern Archive letters that he suffered what was called "shell shock" during and after World War One. The condition is now known as PTSD or Post Traumatic Stress Disorder. After the war Dr. Norman Leslie and his good friend Tom McQuesten often used to spend time together on a Saturday afternoon at the Hamilton Club or at the Thistle Club.

One wonders how Tom must have felt after hearing what Dr. Leslie had endured and had reported for himself and for others. A letter dated March 26, 1947, from Mel Smith to Tom McQuesten, mentions Dr. Leslie in failing health: *I have heard nothing further since I left Toronto as to the health of our friend Dr. Leslie, and I trust he is quite himself again. This also applies to many others of his type that we know in Hamilton.* The phrase *"of his type"* may be referring to a "shell shock" condition that Leslie and others suffered, during and after the war. Norman Leslie never went back to medicine after his war experiences at the French Front.

A *Spectator* article dated July 13, 1938 states: *Dr. N.V. Leslie fills in vacancy in Hydro body. Prominent Hamilton physician and war veteran to succeed John Newlands.* Tom likely recommended Leslie for this position, using his influence with government and with Hydro. Also, through Tom's recommendation, Dr. Leslie became a Niagara Falls Bridge Commissioner from July 22, 1941 until January 9, 1947. No doubt Leslie would have assisted in many of Tom's bridge-building projects. Rev. Calvin McQuesten, in his diary, mentions Dr. Norman Leslie as applying to be a Commissioner and as having received the position.

After reading Dr. Leslie's letters and perceiving his condition on returning, Tom may have been relieved that he had not been able to enlist. The Hon. Thomas Baker McQuesten went on to create wonderful benefits for Hamilton, Niagara, and all of Ontario. To name just a few: Gage Park; The High Level Bridge (later named for McQuesten); McMaster University; Royal Botanical Gardens; Queen Elizabeth Highway; Niagara Parkway and Gardens; Carillon Tower; Rainbow Bridge; Blue Water Bridge and Thousand Islands Bridge, and many historical restorations of forts and buildings. The three international bridges were part of Tom's efforts to cement the peace between nations. His maternal grandfather, Rev. Thomas Baker, had participated in the war of 1812 on the HMS *St. Lawrence*—so Tom may have been greatly affected in his emphasis on peace by his grandfather as well as by his friend Dr. Norman Leslie.

RUBY BAKER MCQUESTEN: RUBY'S TRAGIC LIFE STORY AND THWARTED ROMANCE

Ruby was a lot like her name: beautiful, charming and precious. Ruby was only nine years old in 1888 when her father, Isaac McQuesten, died "unexpectedly." He was bankrupt and left his wife with large liabilities. Of course, the rumours of suicide were rife—especially because it was known that he was being treated for addictions, alcoholism and mental illness at Homewood Hospital in Guelph by Dr. Lett. Some say he committed suicide because of his bankruptcy, which was not uncommon at that time. To make matters worse, there were no social benefits available in those days, so his family was truly impoverished. His death certificate, signed by his doctor, gives the cause of death as "COMA."

Isaac died at age 41. Mary Baker McQuesten was left widowed and impoverished, with six children between the ages of 14 and 2. After Isaac's death, Mary gradually assessed each child for potential to restore the family to its previous solvency and social status. She saw promise in both Ruby at nine and Thomas at age six. But Ruby was a girl and these were Victorian times; as a woman, her career choices and income potential would be severely limited. So the expectations fell upon Thomas, who was more likely to end up in a lucrative profession. That is what Mary hoped for him and for the family; his father had been a lawyer, his grandfather had been a doctor and, although doctors at the time did not earn large salaries, his grandfather had become a wealthy and successful industrialist, thereby amassing a fortune, which Isaac lost.

It is not too melodramatic to say that Ruby was sacrificed for the family cause. Ruby was articulate, scholarly and artistic. She also had a generous, loving and caring nature.

Mary decided that Ruby should train to become a teacher, and at age twenty Ruby took a position at the Presbyterian Ladies' College in Ottawa. For eight years, in a drafty old school, she endured long hours of teaching and nursing sick students. She suffered homesickness and failing health, and received meagre pay, most of which she sent home to pay for Tom's education. She earned $5.99 per week and received her board. Tom's tuition was $250.00 per year with extra for exams at the University of Toronto. When Ruby's earnings were factored up to the number of work weeks it came to just enough to pay for Tom's tuition and his exams.

EXCERPTED COPIES OF SOME OF RUBY'S LETTERS ABOUT SENDING MONEY TO TOM OR HOME

[W-MCP2-4.097; 1905/2/13] To Tom from his sister Ruby: *I'm just sending you a little of that poor stuff necessary sometimes, as the brain cannot stalk along by itself, no matter how fine it be. It is just made out for the ordinary post I fancy as I never heard how the last one worked.*

Note the slight bit of chastisement in the last line; Ruby is never rude or demanding.

[W-MCP2-4.055; 1905/3/10] To Tom from his sister Ruby: *Mama said that if I sent you $26 you would give Cal $15 & next time you would need more money yourself. So, you can see Cal & give him his and tell him he will get a letter very soon, probably by Monday.*

[W5996; 1905/10/8] To mother from Ruby: *And then I feel thankful that I can do a little to help things along. Your letter came at noon & I was so glad to get it. I will explain to Mrs. Ross and see what can be arranged right away. Poor old Tom! I'm sure he understands how things are & it truly made me feel quite happy to think I could be of some use, though really Mother dearest I'm not doing more than you all, for you save money if I make it and Hilda and Mary are as hard working as I.*

[W4263; 1902/12/3] To Calvin from his sister Ruby: *I suppose Mither told you I'm minus 6 weeks pay $34 but it is to be taken off, part off of each payment after Xmas & we are to have all our money up to Xmas. So, I expect a $34 coming in—but after I've taken out fare back to Ottawa & something to keep me going till Feb. there will be* *only about $20—however it will help us along... Really, I get as excited as ever when I think of Xmas coming & you coming home, Hurrah — won't it be jolly? We are poor but I guess it must be the Irish in us that makes us most joyful & hilarious on occasions!*

This letter illustrates the financial condition of the family in 1902, twelve years after the sudden death and bankruptcy of their father, Isaac [W2511, W2520]. It is obvious from this letter that the family is poor and that they rely on Ruby's income.

Ruby and her brother Calvin, the eldest son, were kindred spirits, and she often confides in him about her homesickness and how much she misses the family. In spite of her poor health, her letters are always cheerful, affectionate and witty, full of interesting comments on lectures at Ottawa, books, religion or the progress of one of her many paintings. She was an accomplished artist and her work was reviewed as exceptional. There are at least sixty-five of her paintings and pyrography at Whitehern. (Pyrography is wood-burning as an art, or what her mother called "poker work.")

Right: Photo of Ruby as a school teacher (Courtesy Whitehern)

Ruby met David Ross in Ottawa. His mother was the principal at Ruby's school and his sisters were teachers there. He proposed to Ruby in 1906 when he was 24 and she was 27, which was already past the ideal marriageable age for a woman, by Victorian standards. David popped the question while visiting Ruby and her family on a holiday; but Ruby's mother, Mary McQuesten, would have no part of it. She said that David was too young, had not yet established himself, and his financial prospects were not good. Not only that, Mary railed, but David was irresponsible and dishonourable to his mother and sisters for even thinking of marriage himself while they were busy working to support themselves: "*his mother a poor worn-out looking woman.*"

As for David's plan to go out west as a surveyor and homesteader, this was completely unacceptable to Mary, especially since David was planning to go west and north, build a log cabin, take

David Ross proposed to Ruby in Aug. 1906, but mother did not approve.

David was 24   Ruby was 27

along his mother and sisters and wife, Ruby, and adopt the children of another sister. This did not suit Mary's sensibilities and high hopes for her children. Ruby's appeals to her mother fell on deaf ears. Mary put an end to the relationship and extracted a promise that they would stay apart and not communicate for two years. She conveniently failed to mention that it would be exactly two years before Tom would graduate and begin earning a salary, so that Ruby's financial assistance would then no longer be needed

Ruby's health continued its steady decline. Letters home to her mother and brothers chronicled the course of her illness: the initial outbreak of "grippe" at the school, the recurring episodes, and the early diagnosis as bronchitis. In 1907, just as Tom graduated from law school, Ruby had to give up teaching and was sent out west to Calgary for a "rest cure" in the fresh air. She stayed over the winter, as her cough grew steadily worse. She had been told that *"the cold is good for it."*

Despite the promise she'd made to her mother, Ruby had continued her relationship with David in secret. When Mary found out, she was furious. She claimed *"heart trouble"* and laid the blame directly on Ruby's already frail shoulders. Guilt was a powerful force in the family, and duty and self-sacrifice were the models of moral behaviour—especially since Mary herself had made so many sacrifices for her children, for Whitehern, and for her missionary work at MacNab Street Presbyterian church (WFMS, Women's Foreign Missionary Society).

We have some evidence that Ruby and David communicated while she was in Calgary. It seems that a letter had gone astray; Mother saw it and raised an alarm that Ruby had broken her word to her mother. Ruby then wrote to Calvin, indicating that he had been informed about David: *Did Mama tell you that a letter I had sent to you in Aug. had been returned to me from the dead letter office[?] It had your address on in full & I would rather that any other letter had gone astray. You must have wondered at not receiving it until the enclosed. However, I'll finish the process & cremate the whole business. Thank you for answering my last letter so completely. It eased my mind as after receiving this one from the dead letter office I would have been wondering about the fate of the other.*

This is a significant letter and a tantalizing bit of news about missing letters—and how we wish we had those letters that Ruby "cremated." We have NO letters from Ruby between July 22, 1908 [W6229, W-MCP3-05-003] and September 8, 1908 [W6266], except for one brief letter from Ruby to her sister, Hilda, on August 15 [Box 03-001]. The missing letters for this period are likely the ones that were "cremated" or destroyed. We have some clues that lead to correspondence and possibly contact between Ruby and David Ross: (1) Ruby's letter of September 10, 1908 to Calvin indicates that Cal had written to her to suggest that she visit David and the Rosses [W6281]. (2) In her letter to Cal of October 1, 1908, she states that: *it's all finally off between David and myself. It was his decision and everything is now over and done. So, you can burn this letter & we'll not mention the subject again* [W6302]—which certainly indicates that there had been communication.

The letter that Ruby mentions as having gone astray, and which landed in her mother's possession, is likely a letter which gave away some details about a secret relationship between herself and David.

It is a mystery how a letter from Ruby in Calgary to Calvin in Toronto ended up in the dead letter office in Hamilton and subsequently in Ruby's mother's hands, unless someone in the dead letter office in Toronto knew the McQuesten name and sent it along to Hamilton. The other possibility is that Calvin actually, or inadvertently, gave the letter to his mother, or she found it among his laundry that he had brought home, and she pretended it had gone to the dead letter office.

Another mystery is that there are NO letters from the family TO Ruby in the archive, yet she often comments to thank Tom or Calvin, etc., for their letters. Did she destroy them and, if so, why? Were they destroyed later to remove any possibility of TB germs being transmitted? Yet we have so many of the letters from Ruby to the family and they would have been even more TB germ-laden. It is possible that Ruby cremated some of the family letters along with the letters from David Ross—but that is not likely, since the family were so careful to save all letters. We can only speculate on the reasons, unless with research some of the letters come to light, which is unlikely.

In Mary's defence, the family was in dire financial straits at the time and there was no relief in sight. She worried constantly about losing Whitehern, and even rented out Whitehern for a time to the Hamilton Club in 1907 while the family went to live in Oakville. Also, the medical bills were relentless. Ruby's "bronchitis" was never diagnosed as "tuberculosis," for that was a taboo word stirring fear in all. She was sent to Calgary in 1907, and then to a sanatorium in Muskoka. This is curious, since Hamilton's treatment centre for tuberculosis had opened in 1906 and was proving successful in treating the disease. Ruby was finally sent to a cottage on the Hamilton Mountain where the family could visit, and Tom did his best to help to keep her comfortable there until she died in 1911.

Also, at that time, Edna's health had failed. She had suffered a mental breakdown and was sent to Montreal for treatment along with a nurse. We have named Edna "the madwoman in the attic" because the family tried to keep Edna's mental condition a secret, and Hilda cautions Calvin about Edna's breakdown: *I warned him that if people become too inquisitive about Edna to say that the nurse came from Montreal; and that Edna went back with her as the Doctor advised change of scenery and invigorating air. We do not mention her name unless people ask after her particularly* [W5430, October 19, 1905].

During this period daughter Mary was receiving regular treatments in Toronto for a skin condition on her face; and mother Mary had health problems too. These were all troubling medical expenses. Mary's claim of a weak heart seems to have been a matriarchal last resort to keep Ruby's salary coming in, and her reason for objecting to Ruby's marriage was likely the unspoken one: that Ruby's income was needed to put Tom through university for the final two years.

Tom was the family's only hope for relief from its desperate financial woes. This was especially true since Calvin, the eldest son, who was somewhat physically disabled and mentally fragile, hadn't yet established himself financially, and never really did so. As noted, Ruby, on occasion, was sending money to him as well.

Ruby McQuesten is a doubly tragic figure of sacrifice. She was sent away from her beloved home and family to earn money for Tom's education. She was denied marriage, and gradually sickened and died of tuberculosis, although that word is never used. Tom was always grateful to his sister and likely felt responsible for her situation. He visited her regularly and he helped to rent a cottage for her on the Hamilton Mountain during her final months. Tom became the successful lawyer and politician. Ruby remained cheerful to the end, dying in 1911 at the age of 31. She was buried in the family plot at Hamilton Cemetery and was then forgotten. Ruby, who made it all possible for the McQuestens, has remained in relative obscurity; she is the sacrificial virgin in a Victorian drama.

Ruby's paintings are at Whitehern today. Two of her paintings are included in this book. Above: Ruby's "Violin" (Courtesy Whitehern).

*Above: "The Tea Party"
(a painting by Ruby).
Left: Ruby Baker
McQuesten with rose
(Both Courtesy Whitehern).*

Left: William Lyon Mackenzie (Courtesy Wikimedia).
Right: Sir Isaac Buchanan (Courtesy Toronto Public Library).

THE REBELLION OF UPPER CANADA, DECEMBER 7, 1837: WILLIAM LYON MACKENZIE AND SIR ISAAC BUCHANAN

William Lyon Mackenzie (1795–1861) was born in Scotland and came to Upper Canada after the War of 1812. He published "The Colonial Advocate," a newspaper that was strongly pro-government reform. Mackenzie wrote many articles objecting to the government and demanding change. His dream was an American-style democracy. In 1837, frustrated by Britain's refusal to begin democratic changes, he gathered supporters in an effort to make things happen faster. Since his written protests had come to no avail, he had decided that open rebellion would be necessary.

Isaac Buchanan (1810–1883) was the owner of the Auchmar estate on the Hamilton Mountain at the corner of Fennel Avenue and West 5th Street. He was a wealthy wholesaler and retailer with establishments in Scotland, Toronto and Hamilton. He was one of the most influential men in Upper Canada at the time of William Lyon Mackenzie's Rebellion in 1837–38. Buchanan and Mackenzie had some of the same reform goals; however, Buchanan did not advocate violent rebellion. They were both critical of the Upper Canada government because of the anti-democratic and corrupt activities that they observed in what they saw as the "Family Compact" monopoly. On December 7, 1837, Mackenzie gathered some reform supporters together at Montgomery's Tavern in Toronto and decided to march down Yonge Street to attempt to overthrow the government. Unfortunately for Mackenzie, his reformers were poorly organized and he hesitated too long while he wrote yet another treatise to fire up his men.

In the delay, Col. Allan MacNab and his government supporters were able to organize to suppress the rebellion. Isaac Buchanan accepted a commission in the local militia and served against the rebellion in Toronto and on the Niagara frontier. Mackenzie and his men were forced to flee. Those who escaped were scattered and fled for their lives. Those who were captured were hanged. Mackenzie escaped and fled to the United States. Along the way, he hid in a cave on the Sydenham Hill above Dundas, and he was assisted by supporters who supplied him with fresh horses for his flight. Mackenzie was tried *in absentia* and was exiled with other reformers. In the United States he became a citizen but was finally tried and jailed for anti-neutrality activities. He served a sentence for a year but was soured on the U.S. system thereafter. Being an inveterate reformer, he eventually found that any form of government that he encountered, needed reforming. As Mackenzie languished in exile, he desired to return to Canada.

Isaac Buchanan continued to agitate toward reform by peaceful means. He warned that another rebellion was imminent unless more equitable changes were made in government. Reform did finally occur in 1848 when Upper and Lower Canada formed a new democratic parliament of the Province of Canada and received responsible government.

In the elections for the third Parliament of the Province of Canada, the Reformers won, and enacted sweeping reforms, which included an amnesty act for the rebels of 1837. It passed the Assembly in February 1849, and Mackenzie asked influential Reformers such as Isaac Buchanan and others to lobby for amnesty for himself, even though he was now a United States citizen. The new government and its supporters came to realize that those who had fomented the Rebellion had actually been instrumental in bringing about responsible government in Canada. Mackenzie died in Toronto in 1861.

POSTSCRIPT TO HISTORY: Thomas Baker McQuesten (1882–1948) was an avid student of history and in his family's archive of old letters he read about the Rebellion of 1837. In his grandfather's letters, he read of the threat to his own family, and their fear of an impending civil war, and the threat to his grandfather Dr. Calvin McQuesten's foundry. [See previous letter: C-MCP4-6.193, December 7, 1837].

VICTORIAN MEDICINE: LOTTIE BAKER'S CLEFT PALATE AND SURGERY

Lottie Baker (1866–1930) is one of Rev. Baker's grandchildren, one of the seven children of Rev. Baker's son, James Alfred, deceased 1876. She is one of the children that Rev. Baker seeks to rescue from her stepmother, Maria Mudge Baker, whom he suspects of loose morals. Lottie was born with a cleft palate, which affected her speech and appearance and made her dreadfully unhappy. The attempt to correct her cleft palate, with subsequent complications, setbacks and additional surgeries, shows her to be a model of courage and forbearance. It is possible to see that the expense of surgical treatment is a serious consideration, especially if it is to be done in hospital; but Lottie ends up having the surgery done in the home. It is a Victorian medical success story, although fraught with much pain for Lottie. It was a very trying ordeal and required a succession of painful surgeries, without anaesthetic. Lottie writes to her grandfather, Rev. Baker, from Paris, Ontario, about her progress in seeking treatment for her cleft palate. Lottie writes the following letter almost completely without punctuation, which has been added in the transcription for ease of reading.

Left: The aged Rev. Thomas Baker (Courtesy Whitehern)

[W3363 December 30, 1879] TO REV. THOMAS BAKER, HAMILTON, ONTARIO, FROM HIS GRANDDAUGHTER LOTTIE BAKER, PARIS, ONTARIO

My dear Grandpa:
… My cousin Emma went with me to see Miss Smith. Dr. Beard of Brantford advised her not to have it done of economy as the [possibili-

ty?] of her having to go to Montreal. Dr. Balmer of Princeton who visits Mr. Harbin was speaking to Allice respecting me, he stated that I could go to the hospital in Toronto and get the divided place drawn together, remain in the hospital until properly united; this he thought would be more expensive than a false plate [which] would be much more satisfactory. Allice wrote to Grandma and Grandpa Fussell asking them to send me there ... With kind love to all, wishing you a happy new year, I remain your affectionate granddaughter,
Lottie Baker.

[W3412, May 7, 1880] TO REV. THOMAS BAKER, HAMILTON, ONTARIO FROM HIS GRANDDAUGHTER ALICE E. BAKER, CHERRY LODGE, PARIS ONTARIO

Alice is writing about her wedding, which is to take place in London, Ontario. This letter was in places very faded and almost impossible to read. We have transcribed it to the best of our ability for ease of reading. The letter opens with some news about her upcoming wedding, but Lottie and her cleft palate are mentioned in the final sentences.

My dear Grandpa & Grandma,
... I was very sorry to hear from Johnnie that he found [both Grandma & you were poorly?]. I [imagine?] Johnnie told you he had spoken to Dr. [?] of London about sending Lottie to the Hospital there to have the operation performed on her [palate?], I do so hope it will prove successful. [With kindest love?] to you dear Grandpa, Grandma & Aunt Mary. I'm your very affectionate Granddaughter,
Alice E. Baker

Alice E. Baker is also one of the seven orphaned children of James Alfred Baker and his wife Charlotte (Puckridge).
The following letter is from Lottie's sister, Minnie Baker.

[W3420, May 15, 1880] TO REV. THOMAS BAKER, 3 BOLD STREET HAMILTON, ONTARIO, FROM HIS GRANDDAUGHTER, MINNIE BAKER, 312 THAMES STREET, LONDON, ONTARIO

My Dear Grandpa, it was with much pleasure I received your very welcome letter, and also the present you so kindly sent me, I can assure you it was very acceptable. Aunt and Allie arrived this evening, Lottie and Willie you will be pleased to hear are quite well, there is a prospect of Lottie living with Mr. & Mrs. Harbin. I believe Allie says she can go to the Paris School, for a year or phraps [sic] longer if she lives with them, you asked me about Lottie's going to the Hospital, Lottie was to give ten dollars, money you gave her, at different times, which she has been saving for a long while. John, Allie, and I were to pay an equal share in the remaining expenses, I daresay you are aware there are three wards in the Hospital ordinary special and private. John intended making particular inquiries to see if she would have every necessary comfort in the special and if not, we intended she should go in the private. If the first operation is successful three or four weeks will be long enough for her to remain there. If not, successful she may have to stay the same length of time over again. John or I could visit her every day so I think she will not find the time nearly so dull as if she went to Toronto where we first thought of sending her.

I can assure you Dear Grandpa in the case of Mr. Harbin's groomsman, although he was an old friend of poor Father's and the very gentleman Pa had picked out in his own mind. As suitable for Mr. Harbin, and also suitable as my escort, I may say to you that I know no Gentleman whose company I would prefer to his on the Occasion, but never the less, I am forced to admit there is no engagement in this instance.

Hoping Dear Grandpa, Grandma and you are enjoying better health. Aunt Puckridge I am sorry to say is very poorly. John not very well, we girls and Jimmie are quite well, we all unite in kindest love to you all.

From your affectionate Granddaughter,
Minnie Baker
PS. Please excuse all mistakes as Allie will not stop talking while I am writing.

[W3426, June 1, 1880] This is a brief postcard to Rev. Baker from his grandson, John Puckridge Baker, stating that Lottie is at Alice's wedding but will not be going into surgery immediately.

[W3434, June 9, 1880] TO REV. THOMAS BAKER, 3 BOLD STREET, HAMILTON, ONTARIO, FROM HIS GRANDSON JOHN PUCKRIDGE BAKER, 312 THAMES STREET, LONDON, ONTARIO

The following letter is very long and covers many topics, some of which deal with Lottie's surgery. We have included the complete letter as it deals with many important and cultural subjects affecting the family, including an update on William, another of Baker's grandchildren. Rev. Baker is being informed of William's stock of clothing and books and of William's place in the school. In reviewing the costs John Puckridge Baker is no doubt soliciting funds to help care for his expanded family. Rev. Baker is also being informed about the possibility of finding a church for his family to attend. It is obvious from the letter that the attendance at church might provide suitable partners for the unmarried girls and might lead to suitable jobs for the boys.

My dear Grandpa:

In case of interruption or want of space I will to business first this time. As you are aware Willie arrived here on the 26th of May. I went with him to be examined by the Inspector on the following Monday, and the next morning, Tuesday June 1, he commenced school. He was pronounced fit only for the junior department of the [third?] book. Considering that all was strange to him, I thought he passed his examination well, he has been applying himself closely and I trust we will be enabled to send you a report of his progress that will prove gratifying.

I had intended that till the holidays he should upon no pretext miss a day, but much to my disappointment and his discomfort he has caught the measles, perhaps from Alfred, who had them a few days since, in a very mild form. As a guide to you in giving me instructions what to get for him, I will let you know what he brought with him. One suit of plain tweed nearly new, the coat of which is rather heavy for midsummer days; one Hat, one pair socks, one pair coarse boots, considerably worn. One woollen undershirt, one pair of coloured shirts, and one pair of handkerchiefs, together with one very old coat and pair of overalls neither of which would be fit to wear out of the back yard, and no trunk of any kind. In the way of school books, he had nothing whatever but a slate, and a ["third" crossed out] fourth reader. He says that he has had no books bought for him but the reader since he went to his Uncle's, and that he studied in books belonging to the others. Minnie tells me that he also has, one pair of braces, and one good ulster overcoat. I think it right for me to add that I think he is one of those boys, (of which there are very many) who are not very easy on clothes anyway. So, judging from his present appearance Uncle John has not allowed the bill for his clothes to grow large and has thereby set an example rather hard to emulate, and also keep the lad looking respectable. I shall try however, after hearing from you, to be guided by your instruction.

Lottie came to London with Willie on the 26th and is well as usual and seems to enjoy the holiday very much. The Dr. who is going to perform the operation on her throat has examined it and says that he is satisfied that the trouble can be very much relieved. But is of opinion that as the season is now so far advanced it would be better to defer the operation for a few weeks till the extreme heat be past. She was of course ready to go immediately after the wedding, but that occasion was postponed for some two or three weeks later than was intended at the time of the Dr. making his first calculations, and he thinks that if it should happen that the first union failed to be perfect, and the ground had to be gone over again, it would throw it into the very latest of the summer, since concluding to have the operation performed here, it has always been our intention to secure the best apartments at the Hospital, as it is doubtful if any other would do for such a long and trying operation and it is intended that her food (under the Dr.'s approval) will a good deal of it be from here, although that would not be absolutely necessary but might add to her comfort, the Dr. seems to think it would.

With regard to the expense toward which you have kindly contributed $10.00, I am sorry to say, that I cannot give you a very definite answer for we have not good means of judging how long it will take, or what the eventual expense will be, we hope if the operation proves successful to make the Dr. a present of five or ten dollars, as of course he makes no charge for his services, indeed, is not permitted to if he happens to be on the Hospital staff at the time. But we do not expect that it will in any case cost over fifty or under thirty dollars that is to say in the cash outlay, though it may be done should everything prove *favourable for even less than thirty cash outlay. I only hope poor girl, that she has courage to bear it well.*

With regard to Lottie's clothes, of which I think you made mention in a former letter, I think she has not a very good stock although she is much better provided for than for Willie. The dress she wore to the wedding was a white one which Alice made her a present of last summer, it is a very nice dress of the kind, the material cost about five or six dollars. Aunt Jane had it made.

Now with regard to this matter of boarding Lottie, I have felt much perplexed, and now feel much hesitation about introducing it at all, but as it would very likely lead to further misunderstanding if I let it pass, I think it better to speak plainly at once, and I earnestly hope that you will see the justice of my remarks and not feel annoyed. There has certainly been a misunderstanding between you and I, and I think there must have been between you and Uncle John. Did you pay $100. per annum for Lottie & Willie's board? Or did you pay $1.00 per annum for Willie's board and let Lottie help Aunt Jane, to pay for her board? If the first proposition was your understanding, the latter must certainly have been Uncle Johns, or else under what pretext has it been that from the first day Lottie went there, she has done the entire washing for a family of eleven, and during much the larger portion of the time received no aid from any one; also baked all the bread for the same family; and in short, did and expected to do the main weight of the work of the house, just in the same way that Minnie did when she was there, (and they were only too glad to have her there) and received her board and clothes for her service. If the first proposition is the right one I can only say, that neither the children themselves, nor any one related to them, [or?] interested in them in that neighbourhood thought so. But as the coming six months is all that is at present spoken of, I hope you will allow me to say that Lottie is welcome with us as our sister and our guest, and if the amount spoken of, viz, fifty dollars is more than you had intended or expected to pay for Willie's board, I will of course do as I said, viz, board him for whatever Uncle John did. And though I can say positively, and with a clear conscience that if I were killed on duty to-night I would not leave a dollar in the world but my life insurance, yet I would rather board him six months for nothing than let him lose his last opportunity to get a little knowledge wherewith to commence his trade and I am sure he would improve but *little where he was.*

With regard to our going to church I can only say that I shall be most happy to make arrangements to identify myself with the interests of some religious denomination. I thoroughly agree with you that there is but poor society outside the churches, and for Minnie's sake I should be very glad if we had a respectable standing in some church, for there are not young men any among my fellow employees where I could feel warranted in introducing to my sisters, they are as a class a rough illiterate lot, and as far as church was concerned we have not heretofore been in a position to appear at church as we would wish, nor yet had we our house furnished as we would wish to be able to receive such visitors as one would wish to receive and as far as I have been able to observe, the churches are much like the world in the importance they attach to these matters.

But in preparing for Alice's wedding I was obliged to fit both our house and persons somewhat for the occasion and think we can manage now sufficiently well for people, in our position in life. We have had everything to buy for housekeeping since coming to London and I have also paid off outstanding debts to the amount of over $200. So, it has really been the most profitable part of my life in a pecuniary sense. As to what church to attend, we will decide by the time the children have got their clothes. We are a long way from the Congregational but no doubt your name and influence would greatly assist us in gaining respect there, but we would have to move if we thought of attending it [words crossed out] regularly, but as to this we will see shortly.

With kindest love to Grandma and yourself in which all here unite. I remain,
Your Affec't Grandson,
John P. [Puckridge] Baker

[W3491, December 29, 1880] TO REV. THOMAS BAKER, 3 BOLD STREET, HAMILTON, ONTARIO FROM HIS SON DR. JOHN ORANGE BAKER, SEATTLE, WASHINGTON [U.S.A.]

We see that only Lottie's uncle, in Seattle, uses the term *harelip* in a letter, and also mentions Lottie's inability to speak clearly. He does not favour the surgery and has:

... little faith in it. Do not fail to let me know the result of the operation for harelip, together with the name of the operation if successful, I have little faith in it. The operation is of course feasible and not difficult. The result is usually a long bill, and disappointment, as the articulation is usually as imperfect as before in consequence of the [extreme?] [tension?] of the soft palate. Do not allow yourself to be victimized for repeated operations. Ask Drs. Malloch and Mullins, what their opinion has been of the ultimate success of such operations.

[W3496, January 2, 1881] TO REV. THOMAS BAKER, 3 BOLD STREET, HAMILTON, ONTARIO FROM HIS GRANDDAUGHTER MINNIE BAKER, 312 THAMES STREET, LONDON, ONTARIO

The following letter mentions the surgery for Lottie and notes that Lottie is present at the wedding. The letter also describes the wedding of John Puckridge Baker's daughter, Alice (who, of course, is also Rev. Baker's granddaughter).

My Dear grandpa,

I know you must wonder how it is you have not heard from us before respecting Lottie's throat. When I wrote before it was arranged by the Dr. and us that Lottie should go to the hospital the following Monday. But the Dr. afterwards said if we would prefer, he would just as soon perform the operation in the house and Lottie seemed to very much prefer having it done at home [so then we asked?] the Dr. [what?] day he could do [it?] and he said he would have to send to New York for the instruments. But they would be here in a few days. But for some reason they did not come until last week. So, the operation was performed in the house on Thursday but there were three Drs: Dr. Moore and his father, and Dr. Stevenson, they were about three quarters of an hour working on her throat, but she bore it bravely. The Drs. all complimented her on her good behaviour, and old Dr. Moore said, well Miss Baker, I have performed a good many operations similar to your sisters, but never knew any one bear it as well for a young person as your sister, and Dr. Stevenson said if it turned out as well as Miss Lottie deserved that it should, it was sure to be a success. And we all hope it will. The poor girl is getting quite weak as she cannot eat anything but takes beef tea and milk with a teaspoon. We have her bed downstairs in the front room as it is much easier to keep the room an even temperature, than any of the others. I have had to sit up a good part of every night as John is very busy just now and away nearly all the time. Willie is a very good boy and helps me all he can but he has quite long hours from seven until six. He had a long letter from Allie last week, they were in Philadelphia when she wrote, but intended having to go further South as soon as the holidays were over. They seem to be enjoying their trip very much. [Alice (Allie) married Edward Harbin on May 26, 1880. See W3429 for John P. Baker's account of the wedding.]

Miss Harbin was married the seventeenth of last month. She sent us a nice piece of wedding cake. I was rather surprised that she sent the cake but very much pleased as Bessie and I were always the best of friends. You know dear grandpa that we have been without a regular minister since Mr. Wallace left the church, but we have had very nice sermons from your friend Mr. Robertson in name. Willie thinks him very much like Grandpa Baker and likes him accordingly. But they have secured a very eloquent minister now but who has been preaching in Newmarket. I hope we will all like him as much as most of them [expect to?]. Now dear grandpa, I think I have told you all, so will conclude wishing you a very happy New Year. And hoping Grandmama's health is much better than when we last heard from you.

Believe me, Your Granddaughter, Minnie Baker

[W3506, January 11, 1881] TO REV. THOMAS BAKER, 3 BOLD STREET, HAMILTON, ONTARIO FROM HIS GRANDDAUGHTER MINNIE BAKER, 312 THAMES STREET, LONDON, ONTARIO

My Dear Grandpa, your letter dated the sixth was gladly received. In it you requested me to let you know occasionally how Lottie was progressing. I am very sorry to have to tell you that the stitches have all given way, leaving her throat almost the same as it was before the operation was performed. The Dr. seemed very much disappointed as Lottie had borne it so well. He had been able to do his part so thoroughly that he had great hopes of it uniting without any further trouble. But they say it is nothing unusual to have to do it over several times. Of course, Lottie's throat is still very sore, and they can do nothing until it is thoroughly healed. Then the Dr. prefers trying the operation over again. Poor Lottie feels almost discouraged. When she found that the last stitch had given away she turned her face to the wall and cried nearly all morning. You know dear Grandpa she was weak, as she had not taken any nourishment except milk and a very little beef tea for five days. And during that time, she did not speak one word. And it seemed almost more than the poor girl would bear, to think of having to go through it all again. But she is getting quite strong again. And has fully made up her mind to have it done over again. The Dr. thinks her throat will not be well enough until towards the end of next week. I will let you know as soon as it is done again.

Jimmie as been very poorly the last three or four days. He has just been asking me, who I am writing to. I told him Grandpa. He says well Auntie you ask Grandpa if Santa Claus put any thing in his stocking, he also wants me to tell you all he got, but I do not think it will be very interesting.

You have perhaps seen by the papers, that Mr. Hunter our new minister has been quite sick ever since they removed to London. Which was a week ago last Thursday. There was a very large congregation at church on Sunday. Some were very much disappointed at Mr. Hunter not being able to preach. Lottie received a letter from Maud last week. [Maud, another grandchild of Rev. Baker's, went to live in England to live with her paternal grandmother, Mrs. Fussell.] *She said they have only had one snow storm there this winter and that did not last more than half a day. She says Oh Lottie I do wish Minnie or you would marry an Englishman and come over here and live. Then I would be just as happy as it is possible for any one to be. They were all very sorry to hear of Grandma's continued ill health and also Aunt Mary's trouble. But hope Dear Grandpa this will find you all in better health now I will conclude with fondest love to all.*

I remain, your affectionate, granddaughter Minnie.

[W3521, March 7, 1881] TO REV. THOMAS BAKER, 3 BOLD STREET, HAMILTON, ONTARIO, FROM HIS GRANDSON JOHN PUCKRIDGE BAKER, 312 THAMES STREET, LONDON, ONTARIO

My Dear Grandpa, yours of the 1st inst. containing post office order for thirty dollars was duly received. I am sorry to say that Minnie & James Alfred are far from well. Lottie in general health has not been quite as well as usual, Willie had a day or two of indisposition about a week ago but seems better now. My own health is very indifferent.

With regard to Lottie's throat, I am sorry to say that only one of the three stitches have succeeded in uniting the part they drew together, we had for some time reason to hope for a better success than this but a fit of coughing, which the irritation of the parts make it very difficult to suppress must have torn out the two upper stitches, the bottom one appears to have united thoroughly and I believe the Doctors still have faith that they will complete the operation if Lottie can bear it. They are coming to perform another portion of it tomorrow or next day, the result of which we will communicate to you as soon as it is known. Hoping that grandma is no worse and with kindest love to her and yourself.

I remain, Your Affec' G'dson, John P. Baker

[W3532, March 22, 1881] TO REV. THOMAS BAKER, 3 BOLD STREET, HAMILTON, ONTARIO, FROM HIS GRANDDAUGHTER MINNIE BAKER, 312 THAMES STREET, LONDON, ONTARIO

My Dear Grandpa, I know you must be waiting for a letter from us telling you the result of the last operation on Lottie's throat. The Drs. performed the operation a week ago last Monday. Lottie was not feeling very well at the time but did not say any thing about it to the Drs. as she was anxious to have her throat thoroughly done before Mr. Harbin and Allie's return home. But although Lottie tried her best to stand the operation, the Drs. had to stop and let her rest every few minutes to keep her from fainting, and after all it has proved a perfect [failure?]. Poor Lottie is all most discouraged and the Drs. very much disappointed. They think Lottie must of had a slight cold before the operation was performed as she coughed several times while in bed and that is what the Drs. think broke the stitches. They seem to think it would be advisable for her to wait two or three months before having it done again. But have not as yet decided that it is really necessary as Lottie is very anxious to have it done again if possible. She is up but very poorly still. Her throat was much more painful this time than before. She had to keep hot salt on her face for two or three days. But I must not forget to tell you that nearly every one can notice an improvement in Lottie's speech. Just with the one stitch that has remained from the operation before this one.

Willie wants me to tell you dear grandpa that he would of answered your kind letter but that Mr. Tackabery has been very sick which has made them more than usually busy. He is a little better now.

We received a letter from Mr. Harbin a short time ago telling us that Allie was the happy mother of a little baby girl. Mr. Harbin says he must admit she is rather nice looking with an abundance of dark hair and dark blue eyes. Its mother says just like its Grandpa. It was born on the 28th of February. Jimmie says he hopes Auntie Allie will bring the baby home with her. Lottie delighted because it is a girl as she thinks them [much?] the nicest. You will be [pleased?] to hear that we all like Mr. Hunter very much. I for one never heard any minister that I liked nearly as well. He preaches special sermons for the young every Sunday evening. We always consider that we have missed quite a treat when unable to attend. Now I will conclude hoping that Grandma is much better than when we last heard and with kindest love to Grandma, Aunt Mary and your self.

Believe me ever dear Grandpa,

Your affectionate Granddaughter, Minnie Baker

[W3671, April 17, 1882] TO REV. THOMAS BAKER, 3 BOLD STREET, HAMILTON, ONTARIO, FROM HIS GRANDSON JOHN PUCKRIDGE BAKER, 312 THAMES STREET, LONDON, ONTARIO

Rev. Thomas Baker, my dear Grandpa, I take almost the earliest favourable opportunity of replying to yours of the 15th of March. That portion of it referring to Alice's movements I find it exceedingly difficult *to refer to. I scarcely know how to express my feelings at her conduct. For it seems unnatural in the extreme, that now when she is fortunately in circumstances which would enable her to be of inestimable benefit to her Brother & Sisters, & that too without causing the least harm but rather a benefit to herself also, that she should coolly decline to consider their interests in the least.*

She is fully aware that I have been boarding & providing for Willie at a full third less than the same accommodation can be reasonably provided in any City in Ontario. To say nothing of having Lottie the whole of last winter & a good portion of this. And now to my proposal that Willie would be nice company for her during the remainder of his apprenticeship. She makes answer that she does not want to have him about while he is training such a trade as harness making, even if she were living in London. And to Minnie's proposal that it would be nice for her to join us in taking a respectable & convenient house that would admit of dividing, or live side by side in a double house, she replies that so long as I am a Brakeman it would prevent her from obtaining the class of callers that she would wish.

She knows that by settling in London there would always be a home for any of the family in case of distress of any kind & she could place a musical instrument & other advantages at Minnie's disposal which my circumstances utterly forbid me to do. And for these privileges Minnie's company assistance & advice would more than recompense. And in the event of my marrying the change could gradually & pleasantly be made & Minnie find a comfortable home between the two houses till such time as she might find it suitable to do otherwise.

As far as my own individual interests are concerned I would just as leave that she lived in Paris but for the sake of the family I consider it not a matter of choice but that she should try to be of some little assistance. I have layed [sic] the matter before her in this light some time since but she did not approve of it. So I have said nothing since the receipt of your letter. I do not think there is anyone who could exercise as much influence over her as yourself. If she moved to London I do not ask her to have anything whatever to do with me. I would gladly advise or assist her if she wished or would accept but there is no need if she would rather not; I can recommend her to legal advice second to none in the Dominion, & the management of her affairs could be accomplished as easy here as in Paris, & surely there could be no harm in her placing herself on terms of friendship & social equality with Minnie.

Lottie is now in bed & right in the very critical part of her trial, the operation was much more severe than at any previous time & we have hopes of a corresponding efficacy. She bore it like the Heroine that she is, & if ever anyone deserved success I think she does.

I was down to see Alice a few days ago & took her for a long drive, her health is improving very much, & I believe she intends visiting Hamilton in a short time. Minnie and Jimmie are as usual. Willie has a severe cold.

With kindest love, I remain
Your Affectionate Grandson,
J.P. Baker.

[W3759, January 13, 1883] TO REV. THOMAS BAKER, 3 BOLD STREET. HAMILTON, ONTARIO, FROM HIS SON JOHN ORANGE BAKER, WASHINGTON [U.S.A.]

My dear Father:

Your letter would have been answered sooner, had it not taken a tour southward, and arrived here via New England and I am much obliged to you for the trouble you have taken to procure the Lancet for me. I have for years taken the American reprint, but it is only an Epitome of the English version. I hope soon to receive it. The Globe arrives regularly, but it has greatly deteriorated since Geo. Brown's death. The Canada Lancet also reaches me regularly. I have handed the $10.25 to Julia according to your request. She desires me to express thanks to you and wonders how you understand her weakness so well. Business with me is slowly but steadily improving and I hope bye and bye to write very good.

You told me of the successful operation on Lottie's palate, when you write me again let me know whether her voice is much improved. I have seen many very capital results as far as the operation was concerned, but the voice still remained harsh and nasal from want of flexibility of the palate, the result of tension, consequent on the operation. I hope hers may be an exception. I still believe a competent Dentist can remedy the loss of voice better than can be done by operation in most cases. Surgeons and operation mongers, the last by far the largest class here as well as elsewhere.

 Seattle is more than three times as large and populous as when I first came here, but prospects for the future are good. Several new lines of railroad are contemplated and, in a year or two our area and population will double again, we have over thirty physicians, who are like the verbs described in Lindley Murray's Grammar, regular, irregular, and defective. I only affiliate with three of them, the rest are too much below par, consequently I am pretty handsomely abused. I was arrested and taken before the Police magistrate some time ago and fined two dollars and costs, for non-compliance with a City ordinance regarding the registration of births, with the provisions of which ordinance I refused to comply, first because the City had no authority to make such an ordinance, and secondly, if they had, I was not called on to pay any attention to it, without adequate remuneration. I appealed the case to the District Court and gained my suit at a cost to me of fifty dollars. They have passed another ordinance allowing 25 cents remuneration. I have disregarded this also and am waiting to be fined again, on the plea that the remuneration is inadequate, so there is more fun ahead.

 It seems to me that Alfred's children are now old enough to take care of themselves, or at least of one another. I would endeavour to wean them by degrees and make them self supporting. I believe there never was a Puckridge who would refuse any amount of abasement & degradation provided it could be in the end coined into drachmas or drachmae, just as you like to express it.

 Give my kindest regards to Isaac and Mary, tell them I am concocting a pamphlet which will soon be in print when I will send him a copy. The rain with us so far has been very fine, not more than half as much rain as usual but the streets are in a horrid condition, some streets are being graded at the present time and the mud is so deep I have given up riding altogether and do all my business on foot which to me is extremely annoying.

 How Isaac can attend to Law and so many other things at a time

I do not know. I find that after I have attended to business and read the Medical Journals, and daily papers, there is very little time left for novel reading. I should hope none of his [mind?] will be burnt. I believe California beats the world making blankets I have some that cost $30.00 a pair and have seen some at $60.00 per pair. But if Isaac's woollen factory turns out good Canada gray I must have him send me enough to make a suit by mail to Victoria. I have a friend who will smuggle it over for me. Hoping my dear father, you are enjoying life as well as you can wish, and with much love from me and Julia to you and all the rest, I remain,
    Your affectionate son John Orange Baker

[W3788, March 7, 1883] TO REV. THOMAS BAKER 3 BOLD STREET HAMILTON, ONTARIO, FROM HIS GRANDDAUGHTER ALICE E. [BAKER] HARBIN, 236 CLARENCE STREET, LONDON, ONTARIO

Rev. Thomas Baker:

My dear Grandpa, please accept very many thanks for your long kind letter. We were all deeply sorry to hear of your ill health. I do trust dear Grandpa you will soon be very much better. I am pleased to write we are all well except John & Lottie, they both have been very poorly, we had to call the Dr. in for them. John has a very severe cold. Lottie is suffering from neuralgia in her back & side.

Now dear grandpa, I shall as well as I know how give you the desired information as regards Lottie's palate. After receiving your letter, I called on Dr. Moore & asked him the question, as to whether, or not, he thought Lottie's voice improved, his answer to me was "yes, decidedly improved." We & all our friends who have talked with Lottie since the operation think quite as favourably of the improvement in speech as does Dr. Moore. For a time, the poor girl suffered very much from the cords leading to palate not being more flexible, but she seldom complains now unless suffering from a very severe cold. Dr. Goodwillie did not lead us to hope that she would ever speak as distinctly as we do, but he said we would notice more improvement after the elapse of two years than we do at present, "she has as it were, to learn the *letters of the alphabet that owing to her impediment she had in the past only used imperfectly." Dr. Goodwillie at the time practiced dentistry & when Lottie asked him if he approved of the plate palates, replied that he sometimes made them but very much preferred performing the operation providing his patient had sufficient courage & soft flesh or proper material as he called to enable him to take sufficiently deep stitches, he expressed sorrow at not having the first chance at Lottie's throat. He said that Dr. Moore had done very well but he of course making a specialty of that particular complaint ought to do better. Lottie received a letter from Dr. Goodwillie a few weeks ago, he wrote very kindly inquiring how she was & if her friends thought her speech very much improved. I see by the heading of his letter that since we left New York he has started a private hospital & now keeps a staff of trained nurses.*

Minnie wishes me to thank you very kindly for the presents that accompanied the letter. With our united kind love, believe me, my dear grandpa,

Your affectionate Granddaughter, Alice E. [Baker] Harbin

VICTORIAN MEDICINE: DIABETES AND HEROIC MEDICINE

The following letter demonstrates just how serious and intractable was diabetes in 1880. Diabetes was a newly diagnosed disease. Rev. Baker's wife, Mary-Jane McIlwaine Baker, died of the disease in 1882 after receiving a scratch from a cat while she was washing it. While suffering from the disease she underwent a form of treatment called "cupping," a treatment of "Heroic Medicine."

 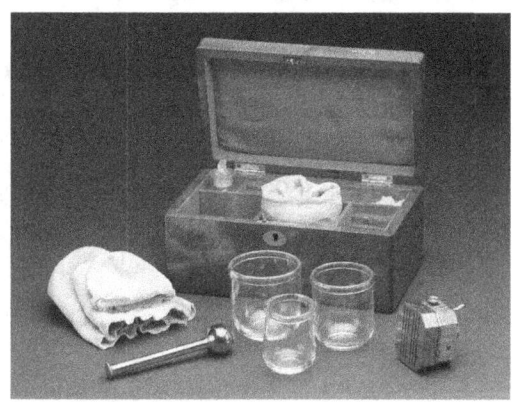

Left: The aged Mary [McIlwaine] Baker (1808/10–1882)
(Courtesy Whitehern)
Right: A cupping and bloodletting set, made in London,
England, in the mid-19th century
(Courtesy Wellcome Images, via Wikimedia Commons)

[W2466 November 9, 1875] TO DR. CALVIN BROOKS MCQUESTEN FROM HIS BROTHER ISAAC MCQUESTEN
My dear Brother,
Mrs. Baker has been trying your suggestion of applying blisters to her side for her trouble. She has gone over the whole area where there appears to be pain, and she wishes to know how long the operation is to be carried on. Is she as soon as the skin has fairly grown over the spot to apply fresh blisters? Or is it to cease with this one application? As it is not a pleasant piece of business, she would be glad to know as soon as possible what course to pursue, since she would like to be finished with

the thing as soon as possible. You've had several billet doux from me of late, so fancy you do not want to hear any more than pertain to facts.
Let me hear soon & believe me.
As ever yours,
I.B. McQuesten

The foremost practitioner of "Heroic Medicine" at the time was Benjamin Rush, a believer in the Enlightenment era's philosophy of natural law. In this rational system, the body was a machine, and all disease was one disease—an overstimulation of nerves and blood. The cure for overstimulation was "heroic" medicine: bleeding, blistering, purging, and vomiting to restore the natural balance. During the 19th century medical science believed *and taught* that the cause of ALL illness resided INTERNALLY—WITHIN the body and needed to be purged out. Bleeding was usually the initial treatment. It consisted of venesection (opening up of a vein), scarification (using a spring-loaded instrument to produce a series of small cuts—sixteen of them) or cupping (placing a heated glass cup over a cut which filled with fluid or with blood). Blistering involved placing hot glass cups onto the skin to raise blisters which filled with fluid or blood as the pressure inside dropped, which were then drained. This "blistering" was used as the treatment for Rev. Baker's wife. Dr. Calvin Brooks McQuesten practised heroic medicine and he owned a case of cups which he carried with him; they are in the archives of the Whitehern Museum today.

Purgatives were also used as medicines taken internally. Calomel medicine was also used; it worked as a laxative in small doses, but usually was prescribed in large doses to purge the system. Calomel was regularly used by the McQuestens: Dr. Calvin McQuesten, in his medical essay while he was at Bowdoin College in Maine in 1828, recommends giving calomel for dyspepsia: *The compound calomel pill or the Blue Pill may be given at night from 5 to 10 grains of the former or 3 or 4 of the latter followed the next morning with a small dose of rhubarb* [W0410]. In 1833, Margarette B. Lerned's sister writes to her and mentions giving "Calomel" powders to her dying baby *"to correct her bowels"* [W0680]. In 1909, Mary

McQuesten (mother) recommends to her son Calvin, that he take a double dose of ½ gr. Calomel and she provides the prescription [W6374].

The opposite of "Heroic Medicine" was the "Germ Theory" which was introduced by Dr. Archibald Edward Malloch (1844–1919), a medical/surgical pioneer in Canada. He first introduced the "Germ Theory" to Hamilton and thence to North America. He brought the antiseptic method of treatment to North America from Scotland where he was training with Dr. Osler. He came to Hamilton's General Hospital with his method, which was to use carbolic acid to cleanse the wounds, and the wards, and to keep external areas clean so that the "germs" could not invade the body. His "germ theory" method was not accepted at first, and he was mocked; however, when other doctors saw the beneficial results they came to adopt his method with great success. His contemporary, Dr. William Osler, remarked: *"In those days the primary inmates of the hospital were rats, streptococcus, and patients"* (*CMAJ Journal* March 23, 1999, by James Kirk Houston, MD CM).

[W3491, December 29, 1880] TO REV. THOMAS BAKER, 3 BOLD STREET, HAMILTON, ONTARIO, FROM HIS SON DR. JOHN ORANGE BAKER, SEATTLE, WASHINGTON, U.S.A.

The following letter from Rev. Thomas Baker's son, Dr. John Orange Baker, gives his medical opinion on the medications used and recommended for diabetes. He is not encouraging.

My Dear Father.

While I sincerely sympathize with you, I feel powerless to help you so far as recommending any course of treatment by medicine. While treatment in the early stages of Diabetes is sometimes of marked benefit, still it is only those cases when time is on the patient's side, the fact that Mrs. Baker suffered from Erysipelas last winter, and that she had been troubled with an [Erysipelatous?] [affliction?] which you mentioned in a recent letter to me would indicate that an only temporizing treatment could be of any benefit whatever, and that Dr. Mullin very justly comprehends the gravity of the case and very honestly declined treating anything else than symptoms as they occur. You may depend upon it he is right, and that nothing is ever gained by administering one single dose of medicine, unless there is a clear indication that, that alone is necessary. It is much to be hoped that a course of treatment that shall be curative will be one day discovered; but till now Diabetes has continued one of the opprobria, of medicine, and the proper person to experiment on for a better result is not a patient of seventy years. Take my advice and leave the case entirely in Dr. Mullin's care, feeling certain that he will give it all the attention possible, and remember that withholding medicine from an incurable case is the wisest thing he can do.

With regard to opium solid opium, meanwhile it is of temporary benefit, it is only in the early stages, when from half a grain to a grain may be given in pill, several times a day, the sugar [pill?] occasionally lessened, indeed its symptom may be entirely suspended for a short time only. While in the later stages opium may do positive harm by interfering with assimilation of food, [feeding?] is of much use you cannot [restrict?] the diet. Meat, Brown Flour, and any green vegetables, are admissible. Potatoes if used at all in great moderation and when the desire for bread becomes injurious, it had better be well toasted. For drinks as I have before written and as you are doing seems to comprehend almost everything. And we must admit that the list is short, and the benefit, at best, problematic.

VICTORIAN MEDICINE: WOMEN'S HEALTH AND EDUCATION

When Mary McQuesten was expecting her first child, she wrote back to her brother-in-law, Dr. Calvin Brooks McQuesten, thanking him for his instructions about pregnancy and giving birth. She was asking for the details about birthing and it is surprising that she could reach the final days of the pregnancy and know so little. Unfortunately, the letter from Dr. Calvin Brooks is not extant; however, its content can be deduced from Mary's letter of reply.

Right: Mary Baker McQuesten (Courtesy Whitehern)

[W1404, March 18, 1874] TO DR. CALVIN BROOKS MCQUESTEN, NEW YORK, FROM MARY BAKER MCQUESTEN, HAMILTON, ONTARIO

My dear Brother:

It is certainly most ungrateful of me not to have written you before and thanked you for all your kind advice and counsel. And I really am very much obliged to you for taking so much trouble to write all the little particular directions for they are just the very thing that our doctors never tell us. At least mine has given me no instructions at all, but I suppose he thought my lady friends would do that. And I most assuredly required all the advice I could get for I don't think you could have found an individual much more ignorant on the subject.

I look forward with great anticipation to a visit to New York ourselves some day. I hope you are not taking too much trouble about that Spitz for us. This is a case in which I am sacrificing myself somewhat to my husband's taste but since he is pretty good I must indulge him a little.

I suppose we may expect to see you in May, remember, however the

Lady of the big house may feel you are most welcome in this house at all times. I don't think you ever heard of your "Paternus" talk confidential with me, when—as he is afraid you never will get anyone to take care of you—I agreed to always keep a very sisterly care over you.

Now I must close as it is nearly dinner time and I must adjourn to the kitchen for a short time; and once more thanking you very much for your kindness, believe me, ever very sincerely yours
Mary B. McQuesten

Mary's letter describes the dearth of knowledge that even an educated woman had of childbirth, that is in spite of the fact that there are two doctors in the family and many friends who are doctors. Mary Baker McQuesten is pregnant at this time with her first child (who was born on March 20, 1874 and named Mary Baldwin McQuesten). **The birth came just three days after this letter of instructions was written.**

Mary's mother, Mary Jane McIlwaine, who died in 1882, apparently did not give her daughter any instructions regarding birthing. Mary McQuesten goes on to have a total of seven children, but one child, Muriel, dies at the age of 18 months. Six children grow to maturity.

Isaac's letter to his half-brother Dr. Calvin Brooks McQuesten describes the birth of his and Mary's first child:

[W2440, March 21, 1874] TO DR. CALVIN BROOKS MCQUESTEN, NEW YORK, FROM HIS BROTHER ISAAC BALDWIN MCQUESTEN, HAMILTON, ONTARIO

Dear Brother:
The show is over & well over, thank goodness. All your lengthened details fell to the ground. We spent Thurs. evening at Dr. Mullin's. Mary felt splendidly & took a couple of glasses of grape wine; about 4 a.m. Friday she had a "stomach ache that that confounded wine must have given me." It cleaned out her internals. About 8.30 a.m. she suggested it might be well for the nurse to call in as possibly it might be something else. She was in some pain. Dr. Mullin came about an hour & a half later. And at 11.30 a.m. it was all over. The real pain only

lasted about an hour and a half. She has been first-rate since, & the Dr. & father say the child—a girl—though small is quite healthy. Of all, the one most pleased is father [Dr. Calvin McQuesten]. *He has been at the house the greater part of the time since and seems exceedingly delighted. Our calculations were about ten days or a fortnight astray, but not more. I hope my pet will get safely through. Everything is all that could be desired, & I only trust it will so continue.*

So, when you come home next time, you can occupy your leisure moments dandling a young one. The most satisfactory matter is that it has a head of black hair. I don't admire red-haired girls. Father felt it duty bound to explain to Dr. M. & the nurse the well-known fact of our legacy from Great-grandfather Fisher. I'm pretty busy today with one thing and another so you must excuse this short note. Will drop you a line soon again to let you know all is going well. Mary told me to write you at once to let you know all is well and sends her love to you.

As ever, yours, Isaac McQuesten.

This letter is an indication that wine was an acceptable beverage for the McQuesten family even though Mary objected to Isaac's dependence on alcohol. (See also [W6043] in which Edna sends a gift of dandelion wine.)

[W2469, December 9, 1875] TO DR. CALVIN BROOKS MCQUESTEN, NEW YORK, FROM HIS BROTHER, ISAAC B. MCQUESTEN, HAMILTON, ONTARIO

Isaac describes the medicines that they give to firstborn baby Mary Baldwin because she is being sleepless. The baby is at that time eighteen months of age. Mary Baldwin's nickname is "Tiny." Isaac writes to his brother and he gives paregoric and chlorodyne to the child, which are both opium, chloroform, and Indian hemp. The use of alcohol was common for children and many children's medicines contained alcohol as listed on the labels: Perunc 28% alcohol; Parker's Tonic, 41.64%; Hostetter's Stomach Bitters 44.3% alcohol. Godfrey's Cordial, chlorodyne, laudanum, cannabis, morphine and belladonna all had a high opiate content, were very addictive and could cause death. In an advertisement the toothache drops contained cocaine.

My Dear Brother:

... All well at home. But we are all about played out with that youngster's sleeplessness. Whoever has her must make up the mind to not more than a couple of hours sleep. So, we have to take it turn about. Chlorodyne was effective twice—taken at intervals of about a week—but no longer. Paregoric, cherry whisky &c., are more likely to put her wide awake than asleep, so the only thing is grin & bear it. I believe if she could be allowed to end her yelling once of her own accord, it would not require to be repeated. But of course, her mother could not hear of such a thing. One thing is clear, she is not in acute pain.

There were warnings in the literature but obviously the McQuestens did not heed them, or felt that their doctors would advise them. Dr. Calvin Brooks used and prescribed opium in many forms including suppositories. Judging from his order forms, which are extant, he often ordered them several dozen at a time.

CALOMEL: A MERCURY COMPOUND

[W-MCP6-1.411, July 14 1910] TO THOMAS B. MCQUESTEN, WHITEHERN, HAMILTON, FROM HIS MOTHER MARY BAKER MCQUESTEN, BOX 166, GRAVENHURST, ONTARIO

Calomel, a mercurous chloride, was a favoured medication used by the McQuestens. It was used as a purgative; used regularly for Ruby, who was suffering from the "con" (consumption, which was tuberculosis, but that dread name is never used).

Mary writes to Tom: *My darling Tom: It seems some time since I wrote you, but there was nothing special to tell. Ruby had one of her sick turns, and was compelled to take calomel, which upsets her dreadfully, but is now better again, and taking her meals.*

In a letter, Ruby writes: *I can't get away from Calomel.* [W6551]

And in another letter Mary writes: *Poor Ruby had finally to go through the calomel ordeal yesterday before she could finally get her fever [down] and is feeling better today.* [W-MCP6-1.395]

The dangers of using Calomel were certainly known and we note that the "Mad Hatter" in the *Alice in Wonderland* story by Lewis Carroll suffered the symptoms of madness, likely brought on by Calomel: "It is well known that in the process of steaming and felting the materials, hatters used mercury and that it eventually caused madness. The chemicals used in furs and hat-making included mercurous nitrate, for curing felt in an acid treatment. In all the steps, hatters would breathe in mercury vapour which caused mercury poisoning and victims developed uncontrollable tremors and twitching limbs, called 'hatters' shakes'; other symptoms included distorted vision and confused speech. Advanced cases developed hallucinations and psychotic symptoms." (www.hgtech.com/information/Mad%20Hatter)

Daughter Mary writes of a neighbour [W4436]: *Mr. G. (a hatter and furrier) is behaving "ugly" again.* Indeed, it is recorded in the letters that Mr. G. was a neighbour suffering from mental illness. Mr. G. was a Presbyterian friend of the McQuestens who was a Hatter and Furrier in Hamilton. A neighbour states that G.

The Mad Hatter from Alice in Wonderland by Lewis Carroll, as drawn by Sir John Tenniel (1865)

used to have bouts and rampages of madness and was finally taken away.

It is curious how humans can come to joke about death and other grim matters. The deadly Calomel became the subject of several dark jokes; here are parts of a poem and a song:

Excerpt from a long poem by H. E. Miller:
If the case was chills and fever, or trouble in the head
The first thing to relieve it was to have the patient bled,
Next to have him blistered just for counter irritation,
Then twenty grains of Calomel for final salivation.

Excerpt from a Calomel song:
Well, if I must resign my breath,
Pray let me die a natural death.
And if I must bid farewell,
Don't hurry me with Calomel.

MARGARET EDNA MCQUESTEN: MENTAL ILLNESS

Edna (Margaret Edna) was born October 23, 1885, just three days after the death of her grandfather, Dr. Calvin McQuesten. She suffered insomnia as a child and was treated with Chlorodyne or Paregoric and/or Calomel, Opium and Mercury medicines. She gradually developed serious emotional problems, insomnia, headaches, and had several breakdowns.

See also [W5426 and W5382], about medications used for sleeplessness. See also [W6373] written by daughter Mary, for an indication of the relationship between Edna and her mother, which may have contributed to the stress in the McQuesten household.

Margaret Edna as a young child and at 14 years of age (Courtesy Whitehern)

Margaret Edna, the final McQuesten child, was an outstanding student and won a full scholarship to Queen's University; however, she was never able to attend because of her fragile nervous condition. The family named her "Oddy," and she was finally institutionalized at Homewood Institute in Guelph in 1920, where she died in 1935. She is buried in the Hamilton Cemetery.

We have named Edna "The Madwoman in the Attic," because

of the stigma against mental illness.

In 1905 Edna's mental health had been deteriorating since the summer [W5382, W5426]. She was taken to Montreal by the nurse, Miss Hutton, and on October 19, Hilda wrote to Calvin about the need for secrecy: *In Tom's letter I warned him that if people become too inquisitive about Edna to say that the nurse came from Montreal and that Edna went back with her as the doctor advised change of scenery and invigorating air, we do not mention her name unless people ask about her particularly* [W5430].

An enclosure in the above letter, dated October 20, from Mary states:

We had word from the Doctor to-day, 'Miss McQuesten has been quieter to-day (Wednesday) and has taken her nourishment fairly well.' To me, this is very encouraging, as she had taken nothing for days and we were powerless to make her. Have been writing Ida Welker, whom I have taken into my confidence, to send her, Edna, some flowers on her birthday next Monday. Have not yet heard if we may write her ... [P.S.] Pray earnestly [W5434].

Ida Welker lived in Montreal. (Calvin had visited the Welkers there, see [W4521].) We have found no letters between October 19, 1905 and March 6, 1906, so it is not known how long Edna stayed in Montreal. Edna was with Ruby in Ottawa in April 1906 but it is not known for how long [W5445]. She started home on June 4 [W5495, W5448, W5477]. Mary was away in the West on a Missionary Society tour for five weeks and returned June 14 or 16, 1906.

Edna recovered for a time but remained fragile and suffered several more episodes until she was finally institutionalized.

Edna's medical records were obtained from Homewood in 2011 and they are at Whitehern today. A few excerpts follow here:

Edna to Verdun. Date of letter Oct. 23, 1920. Cost at Homewood: $40.00 per week, 4 weeks in advance, $160.00 per month.

Surgery ovaries and appendix 1919. No lobotomy noted.

Exam Oct. 14 1930 Barium, no evidence of ulcer but had dark stools for rest of life.

December 1933 home for Xmas, first time home in 13 years. Visits Xmas 1933.

Miss James friend visits often (possibly Janie James).

Tom visits Dec 8.

Excited delusional bitter against family. She stated: "You know, I like and dislike my mother. She is a good woman but has a lot of mean tricks."

Highest weight 165.

She was attacked and attacks others.

Edna broke out with another patient who was also a manic patient and took a taxi in December went to a hotel.

November 10, 1935 hemorrhaging. Bleeding ulcer 104lbs, was given Codeine and Morphine. No Lobotomy noted.

Edna died at 114 lbs. with bleeding ulcer. November 10, 1935.

Edna's healthy periods and deterioration are described in the family letters. She demonstrated sleeplessness even as a small child, as did the infant Mary (Tiny). It is not known specifically at this time what medications were given to Edna as a child, but the medications likely follow a pattern for the whole family.

Mary was greatly concerned about the cost of medical care for Edna. At this time Tom was still at university and Ruby was still teaching in Ottawa and sending money home for Tom and the family. In a letter to Tom of October 1906, Mary notes that Dr. Clarke charged $25 for consultation in the home, the doctor at a Mimico asylum was charging $100, and that Mrs. B[?] was paying $50 a week for her daughter's care at Guelph [W-MCP2-3b.047].

VICTORIAN MEDICINE: ISAAC MCQUESTEN AND THE "ARISTOCRATIC VICE"

[W4327, July 8, 1885] TO DR. CALVIN BROOKS MCQUESTEN, NEW YORK, FROM HIS SISTER-IN-LAW, MARY BAKER MCQUESTEN, HESPELER, ONTARIO
Dear Calvin,
I had resolved that I would never again mention the subject of Isaac's health but my anxiety about him is so great, that I must beg of you one favour and that is to tell me, if you would recommend him trying a specialist on nervous disease and who is the best. My greatest difficulty is that Isaac does not feel he has a cent to spare except on necessities, and he has no faith in any man being able to help him. However, if you could hold out any inducements as to the skill of any physician in New York, perhaps I could coax him. I asked you once, but you forgot to answer me if you thought there was any virtue in this "Compound oxygen" prepared by a Philadelphia firm. Will you be so very kind as to answer me as soon as you received this, for I am very anxious and if anything can be done the sooner the better. The weather has been very hot to-day.
With kind love. Yours sincerely,
Mary McQuesten

Mary's anxiety was compounded by the fact that she was also six months pregnant with their seventh child, Margaret Edna McQuesten. After Isaac's father, Dr. Calvin McQuesten, died on October 20, 1885 (just thre days before Edna was born), Isaac's mishandling of the estate became evident. Bankruptcy was looming, for him and his brother, Dr. Calvin Brooks McQuesten, and he and Mary had a large family and a large home to maintain. Between April and August 1886, Mary required rest and treatment for depression. Isaac wrote to her on August 23, 1886 [W2495]:

Home these dark, short evenings is almost worse than no home at all without a wife ... it makes me sadder to think of a sweet, pure little one like you having to lie on a bed of pain when you don't deserve it, & I have all well when I ought to have something like sciatica in every part of my body.

[W2511, October 1, 1887] TO DR. CALVIN BROOKS MCQUESTEN, NEW YORK, FROM HIS BROTHER ISAAC B. MCQUESTEN, 31 JAMES STRE ET SOUTH, P.O. BOX 167, LAW OFFICE, HAMILTON, ONTARIO.

The following letter is shown here in its entirety since it reflects Isaac's mental condition in 1887. Isaac is writing about his treatment at the Guelph Sanatorium with Dr. Lett and is describing his symptoms and addictions, his "temptations" and use of "stimulants." He makes some puzzling remarks to his brother, telling him of a mysterious plan, and to be prepared to act quietly and calmly when, and if, it becomes necessary to act.

My dear brother:

I should have written you last week. Soon after my return a good many things required my attention. And I found it difficult for some days to get even much ground. Dr. Lett felt satisfied that with care, exercise, there was no need of my remaining longer. He would have preferred three months but thought if the more lengthened absence was likely to in any special degree add to business complications on my return here, the shorter period without such would be of more value than the longer period with them. I returned two weeks ago yesterday, had on Thursday last an appointment in Guelph and called on the doctor. And I think for the next six months I will every few weeks stay over there for a time when I go to the mills.

It is years since I have felt in the same physical and mental condition that I do now. Even when I thought I was particularly well because my brain was very active and I could do much more than I can just now, I can see that that was from an unhealthful excitement, and afterwards came the reaction. But at no time for days together was there such a thing as drowsiness at night, or if so then wakefulness in the morning. Now for weeks past I have felt a certain degree of sluggishness such as was always my natural temperament years ago when never systematically using stimulants. The going to bed every night a little after ten o'clock for six weeks did what I could not have imagined it would. I know perfectly well that if I trust in my own strength and think I am all safe, I most surely shall fail; and I know that there must be a constant watchfulness against what one would be inclined to say were the smaller elements of temptation.

Never before could I for a long period review my past life. At times the bringing of it all up produced something very near despair, and then when it was impossible for me to realize in my heart & feelings the heinousness of sin as clearly as in my mind & intellect I could see its nature, I could not but conclude that a Merciful God instead of delivering me was in pity hiding from me a suddenly felt revelation, which in its inexactness reason could scarcely realize and bear the weight of. I do think that this tampering with evil, dallying with it, in a way that nearly all men seem to do is a terrible source of evil. I feel assured in my own case the doing of that in any deliberate form will *culminate in my giving way to stimulants, just as truly as any one part of the physical frame being a little weaker than the rest, disease will surely fasten upon that weaker part.*

This leads me to another and closely considered matter. I have resolved after reflection and seeking from my maker guidance that appears to me to be clearly given, that I will not continue in any sort of intimate business association with John Harvey.[1] *From the day I first had to do with him his influence has been in every way for evil—don't misunderstand me and imagine that I am seeking any mitigation of blame to be attached to me. I am fully aware that I and I only am to blame as far as responsibility. Nor think that I will allow feelings to permit me to do a foolish thing that could benefit nobody, and simply injure all concerned. But I know now that I cannot rely on his truthfulness or honesty. And while I cannot tell what the exact step to be taken—as yet—is, or what it will result in; I will not be party to right being subservient to any other motive.*

It would seem that no sooner had I finally resolved upon that course than Providence assisted me in a way that I could not have devised, by putting before me such evidence and I could not have looked for of my part in the folly and want of integrity; and by the temporary absence of himself and the party in whom he most relied to support him, have I had this evidence supplied through the agency of those whom he cannot contravene by reason of their relations to him rather than me. I will not weary you with what a letter could not satisfactorily place before you. But you can rely upon it I will take no decisive step without first having you fully acquainted with it. That will probably involve your running over here. I will not give you any unnecessary worry. But I shall not consider your likes or dislikes to examine into & investigate thoroughly all that must be done.

Don't think I am making any mystery now. I am not. But I want you simply to be prepared, when such occasion may occur, to quietly

---

1. John Harvey was Isaac's business partner in the Hespeler wool and cotton mill which went bankrupt around this time. However, Isaac is taking blame for some failure, likely the financial failure of the mill. It appears that he may have controlled the financial aspects of the business and even acted against Harvey, using Harvey's share of profits to make investments (W2653, W2504).

& calmly use your best judgement; and not by my leaving the possible consideration of steps that may not be necessitated, until such time an action has to be taken, then be flurried by being taken unexpectedly. All I want you to understand is that if it becomes necessary to deal decidedly with a man who is not a fool, you will be prepared to act without rashness; and further that I will not pursue a course of temporizing simply because I do not want to fairly face what may not be pleasant.[2]

I send you with this $150.00. I cannot just today very easily let you have more. Also enclose notice of [Dean?] Fisher's death just came in by last mail. I saw a paragraph in the paper about it a few days after it occurred. Next week Mamie Sawyer is to be married and the week after Carrie, Jas. Turner's daughter. I would give a good deal to avoid going to either; but if the seeing people will cheer Mary up, I will be glad to have her enjoy it. A more deplorable union than Mamie's with young Brown I cannot well conceive. If ever the principles of Plato's Republic as to marriage ought to be invoked, they should in this case.[3]

We are all well at home; though Mary is much wearied with Edna, who will go to sleep for no one else, and though a really good little child,

---

2. Isaac's comments here are difficult to interpret. We have discovered a rather poignant indication of Isaac's preoccupation with death and suicide in a book of his entitled *Responsibility in Mental Illness* (London, 1874). The book is neatly underlined, presumably by Isaac. One passage so highlighted reads, "let him then suppose it to be no dream, but conceive himself to be overwhelmed by the horrible nightmare day after day, and to be, as he surely would be, incapable of the hope of relief; what cry would then suffice to express his agony and despair save the cry of supreme agony, 'My God, My God, why hast thou forsaken me?'—**what act save an act of suicide?**" (p. 240) (emphasis added). (This passage came to light when Whitehern's library books were being sorted and packaged to be sent out for deacidification and buffering.)

3. This comment on Plato's *Republic* suggests that the family was aware of the system of eugenics in Plato, and that it may have had some bearing on Mary Baker McQuesten and her decision to discourage her children from marrying. There were rumours that the McQuestens had taken a pledge to remain childless because of the mental illness in the family, but we have found no record of this in the letters. At the time, eugenics was being practised in Canada by the Clarke Institute. Dr. Kirk Clarke was an early proponent of eugenics, emphasizing the importance of restrictive laws that would limit the immigration and marriage of the "defective." Dr. Clarke and others sterilized the disabled, mentally infirm, unemployed and women in the name of eugenics. Psychiatry's desire for greater respectability in the medical profession made eugenic "science" attractive. In 1880, Clarke took a post at the Hamilton, Ontario asylum, emphasizing the importance of restrictive laws that would limit the immigration and marriage of the "mentally defective."

she seems to have much trouble sleeping soundly.

I have met with every kindness at the hands of friends since my return. Though I am told that not many know where I have been, I have made no attempt at concealment & have so informed those who have spoken with me. It may be very painful & humiliating, but nothing is gained by an attempt at evading it, and the knowledge that men know of it will go far should a sudden temptation come over me to cause me not to give way. And it is these sudden impulses that I must look out for. It is one long continuous want or craving. Let me hear from you when you have time.
Yours most sincerely
Isaac B. McQuesten [Isaac Baldwin McQuesten]

Alcoholism and drug addiction were considered "**the Aristocratic Vice**" at the time (1881–1900), and it was mainly the wealthy and educated classes who became addicted … Patients at Homewood Sanatorium in Guelph in the nineteenth century were physicians and barristers, housewives and politicians—individuals of high social standing who were able to maintain their status after institutionalisation. However, by the 1920s, the *'furtive'* dope fiend was entrenched in the public imagination" (Cheryl L. Krasnick, "The Aristocratic Vice," *Ontario History*, Vol. LXXV, No. 4, December 1983).

In his letter Isaac may be describing a condition that came to be known as "Manic Depression"—characterized by periods of excitement and high productivity followed by periods of extreme lassitude, inactivity, depression and insomnia.

Isaac Baldwin McQuesten died suddenly, bankrupt, on March 7, 1888 of mental illness, alcoholism and various addictions.

His financial problems in the months prior to his death were both personal and involving his stepmother, Elizabeth Fuller McQuesten. Isaac's father had come to realize the toxic nature of her behaviour and demands, and had agreed to take legal steps to secure his estate in the hands of his two sons. When Isaac's father died, his wife, Elizabeth Fuller McQuesten, was dispatched to the U.S. with an annuity to be paid by Dr. Calvin Brooks McQuesten out of the rents from the Alexandra Arcade.

DR. CALVIN BROOKS MCQUESTEN: ALEXANDRA ARCADE AND BEQUEST TO MARY P.

Dr. Calvin Brooks McQuesten felt that he had been short-changed in the settlement of his father's estate, and tried to recover some of the fortune, but was unsuccessful. This is the prime factor in the hostilities that developed between him and his sister-in-law, Mary Baker McQuesten. He was left with some real estate holdings: the Alexandra Arcade, for which he was to collect the rents and pay an annuity to his stepmother, Elizabeth Fuller McQuesten, which he did until her death in Petersburg, Virginia in 1897.

([W1652 June 21, 1888] TO W.F. WALKER FROM DR. CALVIN BROOKS MCQUESTEN, DOBBS FERRY, NEW YORK

Dr. Calvin Brooks McQuesten remained bitter toward his brother Isaac and his family for years, over the handling of his father's estate. He wrote to lawyer W.F. Walker and James Chisholm to express his bitterness. In the following letter he is asking Walker to send all papers to Chisholm.

I did express the desire to take the [Alexandra] Arcade & pay the Old Lady's [Elizabeth Fuller McQuesten's] *annuity but never agreed to pay the back taxes on the Arcade. You suggested that, but I went on the principle that as all the money Mary paid out to cancel debts was in reality making investments and no loss to her she could afford to get a good bill. All that I have done clear and bill [sic] by settling with the creditors of Isaac is clean mine, out of pocket, and put into her pocket. Also, it was half of my money that kept the Life Insurance policies going except a little from Mr. Baker. The six to eight thousand a year they were spending was half mine & was not a very honest way of treating the poor fool of a brother. But enough, I never intended to write thus, but as I want you to be fair & square it is as well to look on both sides—and at the same time keep your own counsel as one equally trusted by both parties.*

It is clear to see that Dr. Calvin Brooks McQuesten is bitter about the settlement of Isaac's estate: The tone of the letter is angry and likely explains the fact that we have no record that he ever gave any money to the family except after his death, in February of 1912, when he left $36,000 to mother Mary. He was a bachelor, a doctor, and had a steady income, and might have been able to assist the family when they were impoverished after his half-brother, Isaac's death in 1888. Significantly, there is absolutely no record that he ever helped Tom or Calvin with their education—even though he must have been aware that Ruby was literally working herself to death to pay for Tom's education in law. Likely Chisholm helped occasionally, but we have no record of this.

Mary accepted the $36,000 but removed all pictures of Dr. Calvin Brooks from the house and asked Tom not to clutter up the basement with Dr. Calvin Brooks McQuesten's portrait. No doubt she was bitter because of her brother-in-law's lack of caring for the family.

Alexandra Arcade, James St. N., Hamilton, Ont.
(Courtesy Whitehern)

THE HAMILTON CLUB AND WHITEHERN

In June of 1906, a tornado blew off the roof of the Hamilton Club (an exclusive men's club) and the club suffered severe damage. They considered where they might go to carry on their activities, and began to see about renting the Whitehern house for their club for about a year until repairs could be made on their building.

Mary is aware that they are considering Whitehern and she comments on the Hamilton Club and the storm: [I] *Found there has been a tornado in Hamilton, which took down entirely our poor cherry tree, took the centre out of one of the maples next it ... still we escaped wonderfully. Hundreds of chimneys were blown down ... There was great destruction at Dundurn and elsewhere; elsewhere numbers were killed ... We hear the Hamilton Club is considering our place. Its roof was blown off.* [W5691, Oct 20, 1906]

Following are some of the letters surrounding the incident and Mary's taking charge of the situation to return Whitehern to its previous condition, after the Club vacates. It is possible that Whitehern is finally returned in repairs and renovations to a state better than it was before the Club rented it. After the repairs, Mary states: *It really is very cheering to be in a house that is in good repair.*

[W5800, March 13, 1907] TO [REV.] CALVIN MCQUESTEN, TORONTO, ONTARIO FROM HIS MOTHER MARY BAKER MCQUESTEN, WHITEHERN

My dearest Calvin:
Our house question is not yet finally settled for when I submitted the offer of the Club [Hamilton Club] *to Mr. C* [Chisholm] *he thought I should be assured of more than $750 as they proposed, that should they take it for six months at $900 and another month if they wanted as proposed. So that proposition was sent Monday afternoon and we have not yet heard. It may have been wiser, but I would almost rather have settled it and taken the chance, for I am so tired of indecision and am afraid of missing Oakville houses. Page's Cottages are so very small and*

close to each other. Think it a very good suggestion about photographing rooms and will try to have it done.

[W5804, March 20, 1907] TO [REV.] CALVIN MCQUESTEN, TORONTO, ONTARIO FROM HIS MOTHER MARY BAKER MCQUESTEN, WHITEHERN

... As to our house I think it is almost certain to go on. I was at Dr. Osborne's yesterday ... and he said there was nothing else to do but go on for they all knew already that the cost of building would be great, and when they give us an indemnity of $200, it looks pretty certain. At any rate we will have a cottage for the summer ... When Mr. Mason and the steward and cooks were over on Monday, he decided they would not take attic (which seems too good to be true) but every inch of cellar space. I was horrified to hear the bar was to be in back cellar, had not quite realized that feature, but it seemed as if I had gone too far to draw back, and wondered if I were doing wrong and yet it is just the same as an hotel.

Mary McQuesten is quite distressed about the damages to Whitehern after the Hamilton Club moved out, so she supervises repairs and changes to Whitehern, to bring it back to what she feels is necessary.

[W6012, January 25, 1908] TO [REV.] CALVIN MCQUESTEN, TORONTO, ONTARIO FROM HIS MOTHER MARY BAKER MCQUESTEN, WHITEHERN

Twice I went over to the [Hamilton] *Club after missing things and to-day at last John the Carpenter is to finish boarding up the kitchen and stopping up the electric light holes. There are just as many little things that one has to get right. Friday Rachel worked away and got the kitchen's pantry & cellar clean. Today another woman got the stairs and halls cleaned and the big dining room. The dirt you know has been terrible. Since I wrote you I had Matthew's men up, before seeing Patterson again and decided would be best to let Watkin's man do it. They had the best oak all ready seasoned and would put a border 20½ in. besides the windows all round for $35, it would be entirely* *finished. I could see no special use in a floor all over & after Patterson's work was done, then Ross would have to finish it.*

[W6020, January 30, 1908] TO [REV.] CALVIN MCQUESTEN, TORONTO, ONTARIO FROM HIS MOTHER, MARY BAKER MCQUESTEN, WHITEHERN

My dearest Calvin, we are still going on trying to get settled, and the girls have been working hard to straighten things, whilst I do the superintending of the various men. Monday Ross and his sons with two painters arrived first thing evidently determined to settle things. Once more the library ceiling was washed off and young Ross tackled the dining room wall, which had persisted in drying in streaks, his first coat did the same but afterwards his father assisted and found the right thing; then Ross Sen. the material for library ceiling and it is really perfect now. Just a sunset trick over it all, without any decoration, which will satisfy Tom and suits the paper perfectly… Last night Mr. Gentle, whom I wanted to polish up sideboard &c., came in and I was quite upset to find the sideboard would have to be taken away and need about 5 weeks before being finished has to be scraped and cost about $13.00. If it had been standing on a carpet would not have looked so badly, but the fine hard wood floor was such a contrast. Then the ledges of the bookcases have to be scraped too, so very badly stained by the wine glasses of those wretches. The dining room carpet is beautiful, I think and when I went down to Watkins today, Mr. W. himself said he would not want any note for payment, my word was sufficient to pay on March lst. Yesterday poor Mary dusted all the books in the library, yesterday and to-day, and the carpet is down at last. All the carpets are down now and the pictures up in the dining room.

The new carpet in grandpa's room is lovely. Edna is perfectly delighted with the colour of her room. The drawing room set came home today and perfectly gorgeous. All the people from Matthews say they never saw anything like them. Then our new bathroom and bath and Ross found a lovely border and put the same round little room next and Calsomined the room in green so all that paint is fresh.

Finally, I got to the root of what made that awful smell downstairs. The club's porter was over and I just got at him. There were 5 kegs of rotten oysters in the coal room and he had to open them and was sick enough himself as was the painter first day he went to furnace. Then ice under refrigerator was a lot of rotten fish. I felt better after I knew just what it was, so we have tried carbolic acid, but it is not gone yet, but today I got another stuff from Parke and hope to get it out finally. But with it all think we have reason to be thankful that no real injury has been done to the house. They certainly did very stupid things taking down brackets etc. when there was no need and making trouble but these are trifles.

[W6079, April 15, 1908] TO [REV.] CALVIN MCQUESTEN, GLENHURST SASKATCHEWAN FROM HIS MOTHER MARY BAKER MCQUESTEN

My dearest Calvin, Tom is to try and make a side-walk in the yard out of our old kitchen flooring. I have found a new man in the garden and think he will be very good, in the meantime, I have been making the best of Gourlay to tidy up the yard, endless rubbish left after the Club. Just after I wrote you, received reply from the Club, refusing to do anything; it was a typewritten impertinent letter, implying that I had made a false representation of the condition of the gate. Mr. Chisholm gave the letter to Mr. Staunton and had not seen him since, but Mr. O'Heir said he and Mr. S had both thought it most impertinent. I suppose Mason is worn out and cross with the whole thing. The new club is not pleasing and they are all at loggerheads and deep in debt. It really is cheering to be in a house that is in good repair... With much love from all.

Your loving Mother
M.B. McQuesten

MEDICAL STUDENT LETTTERS WHILE TRAVELING ABROAD AND STUDYING MEDICINE IN EUROPE

This is a somewhat humorous image of medical students conducting an autopsy (note cadaver and skeleton). Dr. Calvin Brooks McQuesten is seated far right with beard and his name is on the blackboard, fourth name from the bottom (Courtesy Whitehern, c. 1870).

The letters on the following pages are dated between 1871 and 1872. They are copies of letters written to Dr. Calvin Brooks McQuesten by his friends, Dr. J. H. Whittemore and Dr. George Moody, who are studying abroad, travelling throughout Europe and visiting various medical centres in the major cities. They encouraged Dr. Calvin Brooks McQuesten to come over to travel and practise with them. Dr. Calvin Brooks did not join them; we do not know the reason. The letters have been reproduced in their entirety in order to demonstrate the relationship between the parties and the complexities of travel and medical practices in the 1870s.

Dr. Calvin Brooks McQuesten graduated Dartmouth College in 1861 (estimate, per CMQPW). He received further education at the College of Physicians and Surgeons in New York City, and also served during the American Civil War 1861–1865 (CMQPW). He died February 19, 1912 and is buried in the Hamilton Cemetery.

[W1321, August 2, 1871] TO DR. CALVIN BROOKS MCQUESTEN, HAMILTON, ONTARIO, FROM FRIENDS "PARSON" (GEORGE MOODY) AND J.H. WHITTEMORE, CORK, IRELAND

My Dear Mac:

It is in Swate[?] Ireland that I am in "ould" Cork and old it is indeed. Every flagstone in its streets and every brick & stone in its houses show its age. We had a splendid voyage with no rough weather and in my own case not one particle of sea sickness. Whit was called upon to feed the fishes two or 3 times but was not what could be called seasick. I tell him that his stomach was deranged by the large Amt of Irish whiskey he took. We landed in Queenstown Monday night where we spent the night and Tuesday Morning looking about us. —It is a quaint old place and although travelers & guide books say there is nothing of interest, I found much that pleased me. Of course, I am not obliged to like or dislike just what others do unless I wish to at two [P.M.] We took a little boat from this city. A ride up our area of the sea, of one hour and the most delightful ride I ever had. The scenery is the most beautiful I ever saw and after 10 days at sea I was fully prepared to enjoy it. I spent yesterday p.m. "downing" Cork ["doing work"?] and there is so much here that a verdant yanker [worker?] like your humble servant, can see that I was delighted with my walk over the city. There are no fine buildings such as we see in N.Y. or Boston or even in some of our smaller cities—but outside of the city proper there are some magnificent churches and Queen's College is very fine. But what above all other things I have seen reminds me that I am in a strange land is the endless crowd of beggars and [smokeys?] In [power/fewer?] and [entirely?] and real Irish wit the beggars are ahead of anything I have ever seen or heard "mind that now". To day we have been to Blarney with an old mine more than 500 yrs. old in which is the famous blarney stone whoever kisses will never lack for words and I think every pat [patient] I have met must have been there. I kissed it of course. The ride to the Castle of 6 miles is beautiful beyond my powers of description even after kissing the blarney stone. It is not that grand and old scenery that they say we shall see to-morrow at Killarney lakes but the beauty of perfect cultivation and that deep fresh green that you can see nowhere but in Ireland most properly named Emerald Isles. [We/I?] shall leave this evening for Killarney lakes returning Saturday in season to get to Dublin Saturday Evening where we shall spend several days before going north to London-Derry & Belfast. We are enjoying our trip well and more than we expected. We have many times wished little Mac was with us and wish so more and more everyday. That I have written you the 2nd day of our arrival is evidence that we have not forgotten you and I assure you my dear fellow that we shall often think of you. It is understood that when one of us writes, the letter is a company affair to you from Parson & Whit.

[W1327, October 9, 1871] TO DR. CALVIN BROOKS MCQUESTEN, NEW YORK, FROM HIS FRIEND, DR. J.H. WHITTEMORE, DRESDEN, GERMANY

My dear Mac:

Your letter of the 3rd was found on my table when I went up to bed last night. Since we left London we have been up the Rhine, stopping at Brussels, Cologne & Heidelberg, then to Basle and to Interlaken where we spent several days. I met Dr & Mrs Tyler at this place. We enjoyed Switzerland very much, it is the most beautiful country we have been in. While at Interlaken we ascended & crossed the [Werpen?] alp taking our dinner at a hotel on the summit some eight thousand feet above the level of the sea. While making the climb the jump train was directly before us. We heard several and saw two avalanches. The mountain sides are covered with little chalets occupied in summer by the peasants. The steep scenery we see in our theater gives very good idea of the country. We went from [Werpen?] alp to Grindelwald where we spent the night, the next morn to the glacier of Grindelwald. We penetrated into it two hundred feet—a cool place with ice all around. We then returned to Interlaken and the next day went across the Lake of Thun to Bern where we visited its bears, towers clock etc. The next morn by rail to Geneva through a most beautiful country, we came in light of the lake of Geneva suddenly & a most picturesque sight it was the railway is high up on the hillside amid vineyards and the beautiful blue water with its picturesque borders far below we remained at Geneva a week visiting from there Chamonix at the foot of Mt. Blanc. We had three beautiful days there & saw the Mts in all their bright, cold magnificence. We ascended Montannent on mules to the Mer de Glace, which we crossed on foot: down the [Mavvons?] Pass to the Chalet, then over loose stones & dirt to the valley below, we rode three miles on the mules and walked nine, I am glad to have been gone, went & done it, but I am satisfied. I had no adequate idea of glaciers before. The road from Geneva to Chamonix is as good as any in Central Park and for the last fifteen miles is dug in solid rock in the mountain side. Dr Moody with some friends left me at G. on our return from Mt. Blanc & came directly here. While I went to Paris with Dr & Mrs Tyler. Paris is the most beautiful city I have ever seen and I would like to have remained there through the winter. They are fast removing the lesser traces of the conflict—the conflict cannot even be wholly effaced. St. Cloud is all destroyed, I never saw such a ruin. Versailles is a delightful spot, not harmed. All the worst ruin was done by the French in the communist scrapple. The city is very great & orderly, more so then any other city I have ever been in.

 I left Paris one week ago on Monday direct for this place now Leipe Aux La Chappelle, Cologne, Dusseldorf, Hanover & Leipsic a ride of forty hours. I found Moody in the family of the American Rector but he has left & goes with me into a German family where we pay our board, tuition & everything but washing for about forty-dollars each. Moody, here & still is suffering very much from rheumatism but has to keep about. We expect to work hard as the landscape is quite a different thing to conquer we shall remain here some three or four months then to Dresden or Berlin for medicine. I have given you a brief outline of what we have done and at some future time will give more detail as we shall not have as much to write about in the next few weeks and more time to do it in. We have enjoyed everything and have had the finest of weather. Dresden is a very pleasant place on a west plain on the Elbe. There is a fine theatre & opera here, and I am sorry for as many Americans but we have accommodations in a remote part of the town from them. I met here at the hotel a Miss [Hikehevek?] from this who was at Prof Hubbords when we were in H. and we had quite a nice time. She spends the winter in [Lufsie?]. She writed [sic] me to come & see her, we exchanged cards &c How is that? I wonder what Bart would *say? I am glad to hear that you have been to Canada. I hope you left your father's people all well. Poor Mrs Coxbum I am quite sorry for her, and I hope she will take your advice. I have been quite interested in the developments in the Ring and hope good will come of it. I hope Ruppermen will get his [dress/dues?]. I don't know what Mrs Gobon & you mean about my marrying.*

I have met very many pleasant English people since I landed I find them very cordial & friendly more quiet then blustering Shaddy and after they have travelled and learned that the little island is not all of the world will be a more delightful people to meet. The effect of the Washington Treaty is quite apparent. Moody sends his kindest & will write soon direct—care of H.W. Bassange & Co Dresden for the next 3 months, yours sincerely Whit

[W1333, December 10, 1871] TO DR. CALVIN BROOKS MCQUESTEN, NEW YORK, FROM HIS FRIEND DR. GEORGE O. MOODY, DRESDEN, SAXONY, GERMANY

My dear Mac,

Your kind letter commenced on the 14th and finished on the 17th of last month was received with much rejoicing day before yesterday. I can only explain this 3 days interruption by supposing that it was spent in the study of geography in order to learn where the city of Dresden is situated. Dresden (I will just state for your information) is in Saxony, but Saxony, since the formation of the German Empire, of which you may not yet have heard, is regarded as part of Germany and hence Dresden is in Germany. For an explanation of the above syllogism see Whitney's logic.

Dresden is a city of about 170,000 inhabitants and is the capital of Saxony and the place of residence of the King of Saxony, whose name is John and who is of about as much importance politically as a dry stick in the desert of Sahara. The political wire pullers of the German Empire, at present are Kaiser William and Bismark.

Dresden has some things in it worth seeing and many that a man would never care to see more than once. It has one of the finest picture Galleries in Europe, where we could spend a month with pleasure and profit. In this gallery is the wonderful Sisteme Madonna of Raphael.

There is here also one of the finest collections of rare works of art, jewels etc. in the world.

The Court Theater, which Whit and I attend 2 or 3 times every week, because we hear there the most perfect German spoken, has at present no star Actors but I have never been in a theater in America where every part of the play is so perfectly performed. There is not a poor actor connected with the theater. If there are no Booths,[1] there are certainly no small fry. One reason of this is, because the Theater is kept up at the expense of the King and all the actors have a fixed salary, none of course being employed who are not up to the mark.

Dr. Sauer, with whom we are boarding, told me that it cost the King from 75,000 to 120,000 thalers (a thaler is .72 cts. in gold) every year more than he received from the Theater to keep it in working order. The Operas are very fine indeed—truly the Germans are a musical nation.

We go out very little as our object here is study and thus far we have fully carried out our plan. I never studied so hard in my life as I have for the last two months. And now my dear fellow let me, as a friend, give you one word of practical advice, Mac, don't you do it!—don't you think of doing it! Keep the idea henceforth and forever out of your head. I mean never attempt to learn this confounded and confounding Dutch [Deutsch]. Mark my word, if you do, you will wish you had never been born. I have dislocated my jaw, broken my teeth and paralysed [sic] my tongue trying to utter Dutch gutterale [sic]—I have wearied my eyes, softened my brain and worn out my parts in my frantic efforts to search out the mysteries of this wonderful language and as yet all in vain. I hope light may dawn on my benighted mind sometime and when it does then will be a day of rejoicing. But should this never happen you must see that it is inscribed on my tombstone, *Sacrificed to Dutch* [Deutsch].

I have 10 or 12 old friends here in Dresden at present but see very little of them, although probably more than I should, as it would

---

1. The writer is likely referring to the American family of actors, the first of whom, Junius Brutus Booth, Sr., emigrated to the U.S. from Britain in 1821. His sons Edwin, John Wilkes, and Junius Brutus, Jr., were to carry on his theatrical legacy; John Wilkes Booth, who assassinated President Abraham Lincoln, was born on May 10, 1838 in a log house.

no doubt be better not to hear a word of English spoken. We are in a German family, consisting only of a man and wife and I will leave it to Whit to describe our style of living as he seems to appreciate it better than I do. We speak no English in the family and you can take it for granted that our meals are very quiet as well as simple—I think it is a great mistake not to make yourself thoroughly acquainted with the German grammar before coming here. I knew really nothing of grammar when I began study as I had not looked at it for 12 yrs. and never knew much and if I had been through with Otto's grammar it would have saved a month's time here.

We shall remain where we are until about the 20th of January, what we shall do after that is not yet fully determined. We may go up to Berlin (about 5 hours ride from here) and spend a month listening to medical lectures and perfecting our knowledge of the language and we may remain here till the last of Feb'y. By that time, we hope to be able to understand enough to go on with our med. Studies. We intend to take a vacation of a month in March and visit Italy, returning to Vienna by the first of April to begin study there.

You asked about the weather here. I have never seen colder weather this time of year in New England than we have had here for nearly 2 weeks. I had no idea of finding such weather—My rheumatism has troubled me more than it ever did at home—I have suffered much with it and sometimes for days at a time have been unable to go out at all. I have tried everything without benefit.

Please write us as soon as you get this for we are always glad to hear from you. I will give Whit. the last page to have his say about dutch living—He sometimes gets eloquent over it. I wish I could have a few hours talk with you, I could give you many illustrations of his eloquence that would surprise you. I wish you would send me Harper's Weekly sometimes—but I must stop.

Most sincerely, your fellow [?]
[Name illegible, corner of page torn]
[George O. Moody]

The following letter was in the same envelope with [W1333].

[W1336, December 10, 1871] TO DR. CALVIN BROOKS MCQUESTEN, NEW YORK, FROM HIS FRIEND J.H. WHITTEMORE, DRESDEN, SAXONY, GERMANY

Dear Mc.,

Moody has kindly left a vacant side of his sheet for me, as usual with him, he has taken the "lion's share." He has read what he has written, and left for me to find some details. What Moody has written about becoming Dutch [Deutsch] is every word true. We have studied Dutch like the Dutch, but I now believe that Yanks will win although at first it looked otherwise, and the Parson had much fun at my disgust & expletives. Poor fellow, I am glad to be but of his jokes if it is fun for him, as he suffers very much mentally & physically. I do not think the drink is good for him. We are in a German family very good people indeed, but as simple in their manner and way of living as children. I do not think the German nation very neat, and this family possess the national peculiarity. We have enough to eat, but not of the 5th Ave. style or quality. I often wish you were with me to enjoy the beer which is fine, and I get around a quart or two every day. Water is unknown and raises the dutch with a man's bowels. I tried at first to drink it, but my intestinal canal entirely closed up, and for a time I found there would never be more business done in it, water would not run in it, so I took to beer, and now the way's open. We get our beer and music at the same time, and they are excellent; a pint of beer for four cents.

Dutch girls are not like the fair ones to be seen on Broadway, but they are of like passions. There are six hundred licensed in this city and more who do it on the sly. My studious habits & the climate keep me so subdued that I feel very quiet all the time, we are to day having the seventh snow storm for one week but it doesn't amount to much. I say Bully for the Republican Party. Are the same [?] year. Don't ever attempt to learn Dutch now, it is no use to [try?] ones time. We have begun and mean to, but don't try it now.

As ever, Whit.

[J.H. Whittemore]

[W1337, December 24, 1871] TO DR. CALVIN MCQUESTEN, NEW YORK] FROM HIS FRIEND J. H. WHITTEMORE, DRESDEN, PRINCIPALITY OF SAXONY, EMPIRE OF GERMANY

My dear Mac,

The mail of yesterday brought your letter to Moody and the World and Tribune to me. Moody and I wrote you two weeks since, which I hope you will receive before this and know something of what we have and are doing. Learning Dutch [Deutsch] *is far better to talk about than to acquire as I know from what little we have attempted to do since we came here. Being like we have not gained as rapidly as we should had we kept more in a Dutch atmosphere, and not so much with ourselves and American friends. It is all very well to say keep away from Americans but it is very difficult to do when you know that friends are nearby. It is also a great pleasure to talk in a familiar tongue once in a while.*

Moody has suffered very much from his rheumatism and afflictions, and I feel that it would have been very wrong for him to have been alone. As for self I am not well and have not been since I left home suffering from my old prostration. While in France I felt very much better and feel that I am on the whole better but the close application to study for three months has taken hold of me rather severely, and about the 20th of January I go with some friends into Italy for a while before coming to Vienna for lectures. Moody joins me in Rome two or three weeks later.

I would not advise any person to come to Dresden to study during the winter unless they are quite strong and well as I do not think this dark, damp climate is very good. We have had some exceedingly cold weather and I feel it more windy than in America.

We have continued working as hard as ever and do see that progress is made that we can talk more, understand lectures etc. better but are far from complete Germans and I never expect to be. We continue to attend the Dutch Club Moody wrote you about and find it very amusing. The last we attended two Dr.'s had a set-to just like Dr.'s over the whole world and they did sling Dutch at one another until called to order by the President.

Christmas is made very much of here and all has been given up to it the past week. Moody and I dined with a party of thirteen American friends the 25th and we had a fine time. The Rev. Dr. with whom we live has had two parties the past week and we have seen quite a number of Dutch men and women and found them very pleasant and jolly. They all drink beer kindly and have appetites that would astonish you. One eve. a famous singer was present and entertained us highly. She intends by & by to go to America. Theatre continues to be our Chief amusement and they are very interesting, entertaining and instructive. I was invited some two weeks since to see a little of Dutch life behind the curtain, and life it was, it was beauty unadorned in the strict sense of the word. You would have laughed to have seen a Russian damsel lightly clad in a short chemise, make for me. I was compelled to talk Dutch and you bet I did.

Moody and I as well as all Americans rejoice at the change of affairs in New York and hope the end is not yet. I hope the Erie faction will go next. I think from what the papers say that things are a little shaky in that direction. I am glad that Ruppaner has rcd. his dues.

I presume that Moody has written you that Al. Kingsland and wife are here. I go with them to Italy. My plan now is to stay several months in Vienna, a short time in Berlin thence to England and Scotland for a couple of months feeling that the last of 72 will call me back to America, but so long ahead I cannot tell. I intend the coming week to see the famous picture gallery here and will by and by write you of it. We have kept very close run but fear of the attractions of this place, in fact I think the winter living not very [? ink blot] but in summer it must be very pleasant.

Dutch living is not up to our ideas, and the comforts we have are not known. Moody and I intend to live in restaurants in Vienna and not trust ourselves to a Dutch family. The German people are all educated in literature but in nothing else. But they think they know all creation. I do not hesitate to tell them they think so and in these little spirts learn much German. Moody joins me in much love to you. After Jan 25th send letters to care of Baring Bros. and Co. London.

As ever,
Whit [J.H. Whittemore]

[W1341, December 24, 1871] TO DR. CALVIN BROOKS MCQUESTEN, NEW YORK FROM HIS FRIEND DR. GEORGE O. MOODY, DRESDEN [PRINCIPALITY OF SAXONY, EMPIRE OF GERMANY

Dear Mac,

I will put a little note into Whit's letter to ask you to put a few of my cents[?] (you will probably remember that I had some printed before I left N.Y.) into your next letter as I would like to use some, and also to urge you to write me just as soon as you get this directing to Robt. Thode & Co. Bankers, Dresden, Saxony. If you write by the 12th I shall get it before I leave but write sooner if possible. Bert has never answered my letters to him written 3 months ago and he will never unless he wishes, it makes no difference to me. Don't come to Dresden if you have rheumatism—I have not used Dr. Danby's letter here in Dresden because this place seemed to drop into our hands and we could not find a better one to study in. When I get to Vienna I shall use the letter he gave me—I find I am gaining in my grammar and hope by Feb'y to be able to understand enough to get to Vienna with profit.

Whit & I have bought you a pipe that will do your heart glad—I wish you had it now for a Christmas present. It isn't made for show but for use. I am very anxious to get away from here for I hope 3 or 4 weeks in Rome and then South, will help my rheumatism. Good night very good fellow.

Ever yours,
Moody

[W1344, February 4, 1872] TO DR. CALVIN BROOKS MCQUESTEN, NEW YORK, FROM HIS FRIEND GEORGE O. MOODY, DRESDEN, SAXONY, GERMANY

My dear Mac, your kind letter came to hand last evening and I will answer it at once because you seem in earnest about coming to Europe and I wish you to understand all about it before you start. I have only a few moments to write as I must go out this evening.

Have I written you that Whit left Dresden 5 wks ago for Italy? He could not stand the confinement of study and thought it best to try and recover his health even if he did not learn German, I fear his knowl-

edge of German is not sufficient to serve him much in lectures although he intends going to Vienna with me after we have seen a little of Italy. I have studied very closely now for nearly 4 months and feel that I need a little rest and shall start next Wednesday for Rome where I expect to meet Whit, at Kingslands and Brewers all friends of ours and with whom Whit is traveling. I can read very well, understand nearly all that is said to me and speak a little, but do not know as much German as I wish I did. I think that after hearing 2 or 3 lectures every day for 3 or 4 wks that I shall be able to get along without much trouble.

Please [do] not mention to any one what I say in regard to Whit, nor in your letters. He could not study and I did not say anything against his going away for I feared if he remained he would break down. I hope he will in a month or so be able to understand the lectures. He has been very kind to me ever since we left America. No brother could be more so and if I can in any way help him I shall do so with the greatest pleasure.

Now in regard to your coming here I cannot live a year in Europe for less than $1000 gold and would not think of coming here with less than $2000 if I intended to remain more than a year. I have been as economical as possible and have already spent about $800 and have sent home for $1000 more which will make $2100 gold. This I expect to last me till next fall when I must come home because I have no more money to spend. Whit will spend $2000 or $3000 in the same time. Everybody says that it costs from 30 to 50 per cent more to live in Europe than it did 2 yrs. ago. You know my dear old fellow that it would give me the greatest pleasure to have you with us but however much I wish it I will not get you here through deception. You shall know the truth and then if you can come I will receive you with open arms. Wouldn't we drink beer and eat bread and cheese!

I would like my dear Mac to see your face and if you do not come here I will see it next fall if Providence spares my life to get across the water again. Do you really think you will come over for so short a time as 4 or 5 months? You must not do it if your intention is to study. You cannot possibly get a knowledge of the language in less than 6 months —This is no fooling! I have studied at least 10 hours a day since I came here, now almost 4 months and it will take me another month to get a good knowledge of the confounded language. I do not regret that I came although I cannot spend as much time in my professional studies as I hoped to. If I get the language it will be something that I shall enjoy all my life for when I shall be I can make use of it every day.

Many thanks for the paper—when we get home I will make it all right, I am aware that this is a poor scrawl but I can do no better now. I will write you again before long. Direct your letters as before as I will have them forwarded.

Ever most sincerely,
"Parson"
[George O. Moody]

[W1348, April 9, 1872] TO DR. CALVIN BROOKS MCQUESTEN, NEW YORK, FROM HIS FRIEND, J.H. WHITTEMORE, VIENNA, AUSTRIA

My dear Mac,

Your letter dated Feb. 21st was received in about one month, having been detained in London until my Banker knew where to send it. At the time you wrote me I was in Rome, the most wonderfully fascinating and home-like place I have yet visited, and where I would like very much to spend another winter. I have had some thoughts of so doing, but fear I cannot afford it. I believe my last letter to you was from Dresden, which place I was obliged to flee on account of my health. I believe all Germany and Austria have miserable climates in winter.

I left Dresden Jan. 2nd spending two days in Prague a place of some interest—from its antiquity—thence to this place where I spent ten days in sight-seeing. Our party consisted of Dr. Brewer's wife, son and daughter, A.B. Kingsland, wife and sister. We had fine times, we went from here to Munich where we visited Picture and Statuary galleries, Bronze Foundry etc. We now hurried over the mountains by the Brenner Pass into Italy, and as soon as we got a little way from the influence of the snow covered mtns. We experienced a very a very agreeable change in the atmosphere and continued to find it more genial all through Italy. Our first stopping place in Italy was at Verona a quaint, old, noisy, and filthy city, containing but little of interest aside from its old Amphitheatre, which is in very good preservation. After two days at

V. we went to Venice, the most novel place I have seen or expect to see, canals for streets and gondolas for hacks. Everything is old and decaying, but very picturesque. The principal thought is that it is a decaying city. St. Marc's Church, Palace of the Doges, are beautiful as are many other public buildings.

Our next place was Bologna a novel city, as the buildings in nearly the whole city are built with arcades through, which are the sidewalks. I have visited an insane and clinical hospital, seeing in the latter an operation removing cancerous testicle without any anesthetic. How is that? Now we approach a still more southern climate and feel quite warm and lovely. Florence our next stopping place is beautifully situated and the surroundings fine. Galleries of Paintings, elegant Churches with monuments to illustrious dead. Rome called and we answered in person. Moody joined me here and we gave one month in all to Rome and enjoyed every moment. A whole year would not more than do justice to the "Eternal City." You know what it contains as well as I, but the personal contact with things so old gives one sensations that cannot be effectively put on paper.

Naples with its beautiful bay and attractive neighbourhoods now attracted us and we spent ten charming days visiting Pompeii, Capri, Sorrento, Baiae, and ascending Mt. Vesuvius. When we meet on the other side I will attempt to describe in detail. I hope I could interest you a while but time will not allow and the subject cannot receive justice in one letter.

On our return to Rome from Florence we remained two weeks and then Moody and I bode the others adieu and gave a very reluctant farewell to interesting old Rome and went direct to Florence for one day. Thence to Venice—which Moody had not seen—for four days, then across the Adriatic to Trieste where we remained one day and the following morning started over under and through the mountains for this place, where we arrived in fourteen hours! I have given only a very brief outline of what I have done and would have given more detail had my time allowed or I had known just what part of the trip would have interested you the most. I will try in the future to do better.

We are very pleasantly situated near the hospitals. Moody is busy some four hours a day punching eyes and ears. Tomorrow I begin a clinical course on sick children and shortly one on obst's. and gynae'c. [obstetrics and gynecology] *also one on Auscultation and Percupion* [sic] *and very like Laryngoscopy. You see that my course is more general. I shall see some other courses but not pay so much attention to them as to the above. Such quantities of material as one sees here in all departments is surprising, and the way it is handled is ditto. Nothing is covered but fully exposed.*

Moody saw four operations for cataract one morn. and you can see from ten to thirty Obst. cases every day if you desire. To give you some idea of the morality of this region, I will mention that not more than one in thirty of the children born in the hospital are legitimate. I have been castrated to prevent doing any harm and Moody and I think you had better be before you send us any more accurate dimensions of a woman's thigh and in the same breath say you went home virtuous.

Syphilis can be seen here by the cord. Bumstead of N.Y. is here and is in one class with Moody. What about Ned Tuck's being married and coming to Paris? What is the truth about Fan Peaslee? How is Grant's stock? Does the N.H. and Conn. elections have a bad effect? Moody and I may be home to vote as our money is getting low. Moody joins me in a cordial embrace. Write when you can and direct care of: Anglo Austrian Bank, Vienna Austria.

Vienna is in Austria. We shall leave here soon after July 13.

As ever, your sincere friend,

J.H. Whittemore

[W1354, May 5, 1872] TO DR. CALVIN BROOKS MCQUESTEN, NEW YORK, FROM HIS FRIEND DR. J.H. WHITTEMORE, VIENNA, AUSTRIA

My dear Mac,

I have just had an idea and hasten to put it on paper. I am not going to write you a long letter of what we are doing and seeing here and shall only mention that Moody punches eyes, boxes ears, plays in piddle and drinks beer. While I look at eyes, see women, pigs, and examine bad brains, piddle and drink beer.

We leave here from the first to 10th of July en route for London, where we hope to arrive Aug. 1st and spend some time there. Now comes the idea. *Why won't you come out and join us. We intend to study in London, visit hospitals etc., and we learn that London is as good as any. You would profit more by so doing than by coming to Germany for six months.*

We shall remain there two months and if you come perhaps longer. Please let me know how this strikes you. I want to see you awfully, and we have a bully pipe that needs coloring.[2] *Vienna is a nice town and lots of sick material, but they do butcher it fearfully, and rough is a mild term to use when you speak of some of their treatment towards patients. The city is fine and showy women and gay men prominent. We are having quite warm weather.*

I have not time to write more and pen this at once so that you will have time to decide. Write me care of Baring Bros. and Co. London as my letters come quicker by that route. Moody is very much better since his visit up Vesuvius but it was hard on the mountain and it has been sick and vomiting ever since [sic].

Now my dear fellow come out. I have a place in London to live where my friends Dr. and Mrs. Tyler lived, a nice place. Oh! won't we have a good time, Roast, beer, mutton chops and beer [sic]. *Can you resist?*

Moody sends an echo of the above and we have great expectations.
Yours anticipatingly,
J.H. Whittemore
P.S. Write me at once here, direct to Barings, London, as I have before directed.

---

2. This likely a reference to the Meerschaum pipe. "Meerschaum is a very rare mineral, a kind of hard white clay. Light and porous structure of the pipe keeps the smoke cool and soft. The pipe itself is a natural filter which absorbs the nicotine. Because of this peculiarity, meerschaum pipes slowly change their colors to different tones of gold and dark brown. This adds an esthetic enjoyment to its great smoking pleasure. The longer a pipe is smoked the more valuable it becomes due to the color change. Today many old and rare meerschaums have found a permanent place in museums and private collections" (http://www.meerschaum.com/).

[W1256, September 29, 1872] TO DR. CALVIN BROOKS MCQUESTEN, NEW YORK, FROM HIS FRIEND DR. J.H. WHITTEMORE, LONDON, ENGLAND[3]

My dear Mac: I am delighted to learn that you have for once remembered my address and thru' [sic] fear that you may again forget it will add it here. Barring Bros. & Co., London until Nov. 7th, after that date I imagine it will be somewhere in America. I am glad that the pipe pleased, and hope it will color splendidly, be a little careful in smoking it for a time & do not heat it. I have one smaller, that is doing nicely. Parson I imagine will enlarge upon many things about me while I am away but I cannot deny that I was overcome in Vienna. P. & I have enjoyed much during our travels and I believe it will ever be a pleasure to look back on them as we jog along in life.

I presume that you discovered in the short time he was with you that he was enthusiastic on the [Eye?], at times he would almost get out of patience because I did not take as much interest in it as, he but as I do not intend that as a specialite [sic] I did not feel like taking the time for it, while there were as many other things in general medicine demanding my attention. I do think Grimes one of the best places to see disease & become familiar with it, and London the best to learn treatment. As Moody has told you the Dr.'s here are very kind and attentive and express themselves honored to have us go with them. Since Moody left I have varied life by trips into the country and had for company two pretty and very agreeable American Ladies & you may rest assured that we had a fine time. I hope this week to take a tour into West of England & shall be gone about one week, that I think will finish my travels. I want very much to remain out another winter but find that my means will not allow of it, unless I can find some person who wants a Dr. to travel with them & will pay me well. I fear such is not in store for me. Where shall I settle on my return is the great question now. Can you tell me?

Speaking of treatment, I do not believe that we are far behind the age in our methods in America. Did Moody say anything about settling in Buffalo? I think he would find more there agreeable than in Titusville and besides, he would be away from the scene of his great

3. No year is indicated in this letter, but in a letter from Vienna [W1354], Whittemore expresses his wish to be in London by August 1, 1872.

afflictions, which still have a strong hold upon him. I do think he ought to be married again as soon as proper for I never knew a man who need [sic] a wife's care so much as he. I shall be very happy to see you on my return and imagine I may be in N.Y. at an early day, when we will talk over all we have enjoyed. I have kept a brief memorandum of every day since I left N.Y. I am very much pleased with the English people and find that personal contact with them removes many of the unpleasant feelings they & I had. The travelled English are like our own people & scold at the selfish & ignorant ideas of those who always remain on the little island. Most of them acquiesce quietly in the Statemen's decisions, while some of the most ignorant [scold?] & bluster. They find it hard to say that they have done wrong. I rec'd the Tribune containing the article about Bloomingdale. I do not think they will make much of it, and I feel that the reporter was [armed?] just right, if anything is wrong it must be reported, and I believe Dr. Brown will be as anxious to have it done as anyone. The reporters or [journals?] in many respects are quite [lame?] and of no importance to one familiar with the [insane?] & the requisites of asylums. I do not mean to say that any of the hospitals are perfect: neither do I believe they are places where torture & abuse are permitted. One of the most difficult things to find with the ways most can pay, is to find suitable attendants.

Have you got [cooled?] off in N.Y.? We had quite warm weather here until the 19th since it has been much cooler and I have had a fire a part of the time in my room. I hope you will have a pleasant time at home & find all your family well. Are you a [Greeley?[4]] man?

Ever yours sincerely,

J.H. Whittemore

[P.S.] I'll bring the pen knife.

[P.S.] of the English French Italian & German [lgs.] I prefer German, although the roast beef here is good.

---

4. Horace Greeley (1811–1872), editor, politician, and founder of the *New York Tribune*. Greeley was among those who helped to create the Republican party in 1856. Among the many reform movements he championed were temperance, transcendentalism, and labour unions. With Greeley at the helm, the *Tribune* was widely distributed even beyond New York, promoting an antislavery policy. Greeley ran unsuccessfully for president in 1872; soon after election day, his wife died and he lost control of the *Tribune*, dying himself before the Electoral College met. Greeley promoted settlement of the American West and is responsible for the memorable call, "Go west, young man!"

THE MEMORIAL ARCH AT NIAGARA FALLS—AND PEACE

The Clifton Memorial Arch at Niagara, demolished in 1968 (Courtesy Whitehern).

In 1937–38, one hundred years after the Rebellion of 1837, the Hon. Thomas B. McQuesten (grandson of Dr. Calvin McQuesten), who was then Chairman of the Niagara Parks Commission, approached Prime Minister William Lyon Mackenzie King (William Lyon Mackenzie's grandson) to unveil the new Memorial Arch at Niagara that was built in commemoration of Mackenzie and his role in bringing responsible democratic government to Canada. In the building of the Memorial Arch at Niagara, the Hon. Thomas B. McQuesten and his architect, William Lyon Somerville, decided to celebrate all of the reformers in the artwork on the Arch, making no distinction between the "patriots" and the "traitors." At the unveiling, Prime Minister King objected to the celebration of both on the Memorial Arch, as he wished to celebrate only his grandfather, Mackenzie, and his men, whom he considered to be "patriots." However, McQuesten and Somerville, had a more comprehensive view of history, feeling that the so-called "traitors" were also responsible for the establishment of "responsible government" in Canada, and so they decided to include the names of the so-called "traitors" in the bas-relief on the Arch.

Left: Bas-relief of Mackenzie reading his protests, hangs now in the side-yard of Mackenzie House in Toronto (Courtesy Whitehern).

The Arch had been designed mainly for a walking public, but in 1968, when automobile traffic became too heavy, the road was widened and the arch was destroyed. This was twenty years after McQuesten's death in 1948. Fortunately, one of the scavengers of historical memorabilia managed to retrieve some of the bas-relief sculptures from the scrapyard. They are currently on display in Toronto, in the side-yard of the Mackenzie House and in other locations.

Tom had craftily included a sculpture medallion of HMS *St. Lawrence* on the arch and it now stands near the St. Lawrence Market in Toronto. The *St. Lawrence* was the ship on which McQuesten's grandfather, Thomas Baker had served during the War of 1812. It was the ship that was a significant factor in winning the war on Lake Ontario and helping to bring peace between the United States and Canada.

Left: St. Lawrence ship medallion in front of St. Lawrence Market, Toronto (Courtesy Whitehern).

The Rainbow Bridge at Niagara, which is jointly owned by the U.S. and Canada, and which was built when Thomas McQuesten was a member of the Bridge Commission, stands today as a symbol of the unity and peace between nations. McQuesten's other international bridges, the Thousand Islands Bridge on the St. Lawrence

River and the Blue Water Bridge at Sarnia, also stand as symbols of peace between nations.

McQuesten's emphasis on peace is also memorialized in the Mather Park which stands at the entrance to the Peace Bridge in Fort Erie. The Peace Bridge had already been built, but McQuesten beautified the entrance grounds and added the Mather Arch as a Memorial Gateway in honour of Alonzo Mather who had willed $250,000 for:

... the erection of suitable memorials to the memory of Canadians and Americans who have contributed to the building up of friendly relations between their two countries and in maintaining and beautifying Mather Park.

McQuesten had also inscribed: *Let the peaceful surroundings of this park be enjoyed by the People on both sides of the water to signify the blessings of lasting peace and that only friendship and good will shall bridge the frontier between these two nations* (*Tragedy & Triumph*, p. 250).

McQuesten elaborates on his viewpoint and emphasizes his City Beautiful philosophy:

The educational policy of the Niagara Parks Commissions has been threefold: First through the preservation of scenic beauty and the creation of aesthetic values, they have cultivated a public appreciation for the beautiful. Second, through the application of scientific gardening they have created opportunities for the study of Horticulture and Botany notably in the establishment of a school for apprentice gardeners, and third, through the preservation of historic memories they have contributed in no small measure to the development of patriotism and the highest qualities of Canadian citizenship. [W-MCP7-1.154]

At Niagara Falls, the Mackenzie House and Printery was also restored under the leadership of Hon. T.B. McQuesten's ongoing campaign to restore the forts and other historic locations in Ontario. The Mackenzie House and Printery contains one of the oldest printing presses in Canada. The house stands today to commemorate both the political reformer and the transformative power of the Word.

*Top: Hand press used by William Lyon Mackenzie
(Courtesy Mackenzie House, Niagara Falls).
Centre: Rainbow Bridge at Niagara Falls
(Courtesy Pierre Andree Leclerq, Wikimedia Commons).
Bottom: Thousand Islands Bridge, 1938 (Courtesy Ontario
Department of Highways, Wikimedia Commons).*

Top: Blue Water Bridge, Sarnia, built 1938, twinned in 1997 (Courtesy Perry Quan, Wikimedia Commons).
Centre left: The Mather Arch near the Peace Bridge, Fort Erie, Ontario.
Centre right: Boys' Residence, School of Horticulture, Niagara Falls
(Both Courtesy Whitehern).
Bottom: Wishing well at School of Horticulture (Courtesy George Burns, U.S. NARA).

THE BIG BELL FIASCO:
THE CARILLON CONTROVERSY

*Rev. Calvin, Mary, T.B. McQuesten and Hilda at the Big
Bell showing the inscription
(Courtesy Whitehern).*

After the hostility over the Memorial Arch (when Prime Minister Mackenzie King objected to the art work showing the so-called "traitors" as well as the "patriots" in the rebellion of 1837), T.B. McQuesten had a further confrontation with Prime Minister King in 1945—this time over the bells in the Rainbow Tower located at the Canadian Entrance to the Rainbow International Bridge at Niagara Falls. In the Big Bell fiasco, King demanded that the names of Winston Churchill and Franklin Roosevelt be removed and his name be inscribed on the largest bell, even though the removal would likely affect the sound of the bell. Churchill knew of King's request and any tampering with the bell and the inscription would have caused an international incident.

Tom McQuesten had ordered the bells in England before World War Two but delivery had to be delayed until after the war was over. There were fifty-five bells with one very large bell as illustrated above. Tom had arranged for the inscription which Churchill had supplied using the lines of the 124th Psalm, ending with:

"To God's Glory and in grateful memory of our Nations' Leaders ...Winston Spencer Churchill -and- Franklin Delano Roosevelt."

In June 1947, Mr. McQuesten gave the following statement to the newspapers:

I wish to dissociate myself from the action of the majority Members of the Niagara Bridge Commission in ordering the removal of the names of Mr. Winston Churchill and the late President Roosevelt from the inscription cast on the great bell (ten and a half tons) of the carillon. This action followed a long campaign in which at least three ministers of the Government at Ottawa tampered with and put pressure upon Ontario Members of the Bridge Commission. Surely it is a most unbecoming thing that the name of the President of the United States to whom this country and the world owes so great a debt should be smudged out on the insistence of Members of the Government of Canada. Mr. Churchill and Mr. Roosevelt have thousands of friends in this Province. Their names are great names and should be treated with the utmost respect.

The Carillon was erected with the money of American bondholders. The record will show that the Bellfounders in England, when their advice was sought, could not guarantee that the operation of removing these names would not destroy the bell. The Commission's own architect concurred in this, but so great was the pressure from Ottawa Ministers that this recommendation was disregarded.

The value of the carillon is in the order of $100,000 and the destruction of the great bell would be a very serious loss. The whole steel framework and bells would have to be taken out of the tower and the bell recast. It is improper that this should be forced upon the bondholders. Ottawa has contributed nothing to the whole project.

Then on June 18, 1947, Mr. McQuesten received the following telegram from George Drew: *This is to notify you that Order-in-Council has been passed terminating your appointment as Member of Niagara Falls Bridge Commission effective June nineteen forty-seven (**stop**) you will receive letter enclosing copy of the Order.* [signed] D.R. Michener Provincial Secty Ontario.

The inscription still remains on the bells.

Mr. McQuesten became ill a few days after receiving the word from George Drew and entered hospital at the end of June 1947, where he remained for two months. In my heart I shall always feel that the Niagara Falls Bells killed Mr. McQuesten. He gave generously of his time and money for expenses, etc. and never at any time received anything from the Commission—not even gratitude. During the period of the nine years he served as Chairman of the Niagara Parks Commission and Hydro Commissioner he received no remuneration.

Mr. McQuesten never heard the bells ring.

He was awarded an Honorary Certificate from the Guild of Carillonneurs in North America for his interest in the art of the carillon. Apparently, the Americans appreciated what he had done more than the Canadians [Box 14-122].

It is likely that C. Ellison Kaumeyer, General Manager, Niagara Parks Commission, in collusion with McQuesten, assisted in preventing any tampering with the bells and their inscription by locking the carillon and preventing entry to the tower by changing the keys (see [W-MCP7-1.019]).

Above: Carillon tower at entrance to the Rainbow Bridge (Courtesy Whitehern).

Right: C. Ellison Kaumeyer, General Manager, Niagara Parks Commission (Courtesy Whitehern).

THE CITY BEAUTIFUL AND PEACE

Thomas McQuesten never married and devoted his life to the "City Beautiful" ideal of the 20th century. In this he was following in the *beaux arts* impulse of the Garden City Movement in England and in Frederick Law Olmsted's work in Central Park in New York City (1822–1903). Olmstead is popularly considered to be the father of American landscape architecture. Olmsted was famous for co-designing many well-known urban parks with his senior partner, Calvert Vaux, including Central Park in New York City. Olmsted's inspiration resulted in the developing and maintaining of that park into the late nineteenth century, and it is still popular today. All of these movements, along with architects and garden designers, were indebted to the *beaux arts* tradition of Europe and many of these architects, designers and artists went to France to study.

As Mary McQuesten had hoped, Tom was the one to restore the family's prestige and social position, if not its wealth. The Hon. Thomas B. McQuesten, MPP, who died in 1948, is known now as "the forgotten builder" but is finally being credited as the builder of parks and bridges in Hamilton and throughout Ontario, notably: Gage Park; the Royal Botanical Gardens; McMaster University; the Queen Elizabeth Highway; the Niagara Parkway; three International Bridges—the Rainbow Bridge, the Thousand Islands Bridge, and the Blue Heron Bridge; and many other roads, bridges and restorations of forts and historic homes, as well as northern roads and bridges along the Trans-Canada Highway.

In 1988 the Hamilton High Level Bridge was finally named for him as the Hon. T. B. McQuesten High Level Bridge. However, he has never been accorded his rightful place in one of the four niches on that bridge.

As well as a niche for Thomas Baker McQuesten (which I have urged and pleaded for at various political meetings, lectures and presentations), and one for the architect John Lyle, I have suggested that one of the niches should be devoted in honour of Chief Joseph Brant. Also one niche should be devoted to a Hamilton woman; I will name several possibilities:

Nora Frances Henderson; in 1931 she ran for alderman and became the first woman ever elected to Hamilton City Council.

OR:

Ellen Louks Fairclough (1905–2004) who was born in Hamilton, and was the first woman ever to serve in the Canadian Cabinet (PC). She was a member of Hamilton City Council from 1945 to 1950.

OR:

Another notable and deserving woman is Hamilton's first woman doctor, **Dr. Elizabeth Bagshaw** (1881-1982).

OR:

Mary Baker McQuesten, Thomas Baker McQuesten's mother, who was a great inspiration for him and for his work for Hamilton and Ontario.

OR:

Ruby McQuesten, Thomas McQuesten's sister, who worked as a teacher to put him through university in law and then died of tuberculosis just as he was positioned to become a successful lawyer and politician.

There are many worthies and many possibilities. It is a disgrace to Hamilton that the McQuesten Bridge has still not been completed.

Right:
T. B. McQuesten High Level Bridge showing one of the four monumental empty niches designed for sculpture by John Lyle, the architect (Courtesy Whitehern).

BEAUTY

Thomas Baker McQuesten, who subscribed to the **City Beautiful** philosophy, had a strong aesthetic and *beaux arts* sense. McQuesten worked very closely with architects (such as John Lyle and William Lyon Somerville), landscape architects (Howard and Laurie Dunnington-Grubb, Matt Broman and Carl Borgstrom) and many artists, such as Loring and Wyle, who did much of the sculpture and bas relief depicting Canadian nature in flora and fauna in the stonework at Niagara. His vision was that Beauty promotes morality, and that citizens would be uplifted by living with Beauty, in beautiful architecture and beautiful gardens. It was a known impulse at that time but gradually died away.

Along with the beautiful gardens that Tom included among his projects he set up schools of horticulture and teaching institutions to help to maintain the gardens. Thus we have the Royal Botanical Gardens school in Hamilton and the School of Horticulture at Niagara, both of which have done a superb job to fill this role.

Above: University Hall at McMaster University, Hamilton, Ontario, built in 1930
(Courtesy Matthew Ingram, Wikimedia Commons).

Tom was proud of winning McMaster University and its grounds for Hamilton. He stated: *We've never landed such a fish as this.... In Hamilton our whole development has been along mechanics lines.... And the result has been, the owners don't live here.... and Hamilton has become too much a factory town. This is the first break toward a broader culture and higher educational development. It was surely needed. Did you ever think what a great word "university" is? —It has never been let down, never become stale or commonplace, always dignified and lofty.*

The teaching of history was an important part of the work of these artists and architects since they all subscribed to the City Beautiful philosophy. Consequently many of the forts and historic houses were restored so they would have beautiful grounds suitable for school groups and families, and for re-enactments, such as for the War of 1812 (the war in which Rev. Baker, Thomas McQuesten's maternal grandfather had served).

It is an example of how far McQuesten has been forgotten when we note that it was finally in 1988 that Hamilton's High Level Bridge was re-named for him, about 80 years after it was built. Unfortunately, there are still those four empty sculpture niches on the bridge with as yet no concentrated support for my pleas to fill one of the niches with a statue of Thomas Baker McQuesten.

PEACE

Peace was a primary consideration in McQuesten's restoration work. Consequently, McQuesten and his associates sought to put the peace agenda in the forefront wherever possible—for instance, at the Peace Bridge when first completed, and the Mather Arch which McQuesten added at the Peace Bridge entrance grounds, according to the legacy of Alonzo Mather in 1941. At the dedication of the Mather Arch, T.B. McQuesten made a speech championing the vital function of the peace impulse; he had these words carved in stone on the front of the monument: *Let the peaceful surroundings of this park be enjoyed by the people on both sides of the water to signify that only friendship and goodwill shall bridge the frontier between these two nations.*

Tom had personal loyalties on both sides of the border, since his family had roots in New Hampshire and in New York. He was personally motivated to steer his work toward ensuring peace between the nations. **Beauty** and **Peace** are noble goals. The obvious means to encourage dialogue is to provide easy, safe and pleasant access between the nations or parties. McQuesten was ever mindful of the reasons for the two previous conflicts, so one hundred years later, with international rumblings of war in 1937, he determined ways of uniting and binding the two countries in peace through easy access of tourism and commerce.

Left: Johnny Canuck meets Uncle Sam, bas-relief at Rainbow Gardens, Niagara.

Below: Thomas Baker McQuesten speaking at the dedication of the Mather Arch at entrance to the Peace Bridge at Niagara
(Both Courtesy Whitehern)

Tom McQuesten often spoke about the value of peace. In his address at the Mather Park memorial, on the grounds of the Peace Bridge, he stated: *May I say this peace which exists between the Unit-*

ed States and Canada was based on a just treaty. Neither party gave up nor acquired any territory. There were no harsh penalties. The efficacy of such a just agreement is demonstrated by a century and a quarter of peace. The time span specified refers to the peace that followed the War of 1812 (*Niagara Falls Evening Review*, June 17, 1936).

McQuesten also beautified the whole Niagara Parkway, which had been the road between the military forts in past years. It had been known as the "Military Chain Reserve." He had it transformed from Battlefields to Beauty.

Niagara Parkway, from Fort Erie to Niagara-on-the-Lake—along the military "chain reserve" (66 feet wide)—from battlefields to beauty
(Courtesy Brian Desrosiers Photography, Wikimedia Commons)

Thomas McQuesten was scrupulously honest in his contacts and contracts. In fact, he paid all of his own automobile expenses for his many trips to survey and to plan his works. When he died he left a modest estate of $51,219.96, which included his share of the house, Whitehern. The man who had administered huge sums of money for bridges and highways did not pocket any of it.

This headline appeared in the *Hamilton Herald* on March 13, 1936:

> **Hon. T.B. McQuesten pays own travelling expenses**
> *Hamilton's Minister of Highways pays his own expenses wherever he goes. The automobile expenses of other ministers ranged from $2000 to $6000, but the Minister of Highways uses his own car, buys his own gas, and pays all other expenses. Since he has become Minister of Highways, Hon. T.B. McQuesten has travelled thousands of miles from one end of the province to the other on official business but has yet to submit his first travelling expense account.* (Toronto Bureau of the *Hamilton Herald*)

Left: McQuesten being introduced by Prime Minister Mackenzie King (Courtesy Whitehern)

Right: Prime Minister William Lyon Mackenzie King (Courtesy War Office/ Library of Congress)

Opposite page, top: Dual handled spade for ground-breaking of Rainbow Bridge. Left of spade: Samuel S. Johnson, U.S. Chairman of the joint Niagara Bridge Commission. Right of spade: T.B. McQuesten, Canadian Chairman. Note two flags (Courtesy Whitehern).

Above: During the 1939 Royal Tour King George VI and Queen Elizabeth visited Niagara and flowers were presented to the queen by David Hanniwell and Eleanor Donald at the NPC Administration Building. T.B. McQuesten, far left holding top hat, provided introductions. The ornate royal chairs, one shown, are in Thomas McQuesten's study at Whitehern (Courtesy Whitehern).

Left: The Hon. Thomas Baker McQuesten (1882–1948) died in January 1948 and then was largely forgotten. Tom was applauded as a scrupulously honest politician and a "master builder." Tom's triumphs represent the restoration of the House of McQuesten in dignity and prestige if not in wealth.

[W-MCP7-1.265] *CANADIAN MOTORIST* ARTICLE, February 28, 1948

McQuesten received the following tribute posthumously at a meeting of the Good Roads Association in a *Canadian Motorist* article:

Hail! AND Farewell

Pontifex Maximus, *chief bridge builder, was among the finest titles of the Caesars, and high among the most constructive of the public works of some of them was the building of roads. In this work the last great empire of classical times excelled to such an extent that there was warrant for the proud boast "all roads lead to Rome"… No Canadian has better merited the title of Pontifex Maximus than Hon. Thomas Baker McQuesten, K.C. LL.D. and in his passing Canada has lost a preeminent builder and beautifier of roads and bridges, and the Empire and Commonwealth a great patriot, Hamilton the peer of its greatest sons and O.M.L. Hamilton Automobile Club its very distinguished former honorary President.*

After driving over the Queen Elizabeth Way Henry Ford II spontaneously paid a glowing tribute to it, in the course of conversation with the editor. He stated that it is one of the finest and most attractive highways. He especially referred to the attractive architecture of its bridges and highly commended its landscape-gardening treatment, a feature that reflected Mr. McQuesten's love of decorative flora. Mr. McQuesten combined the aesthetic with the practical to a degree that is lamentably rare in our race. Thanks in no small part to him, Hamilton's northwest entrance was transformed from an eye sore into a thing of beauty of international fame that gives Hamilton a magnificent main portal, rivalled by few cities of any size anywhere. This is but one of many places where his touch made "the desert rejoice and blossom as the rose". Possibly nowhere is this better exemplified than by Hamilton's glorious rock garden which formerly was an enormous and unsightly gravel pit. To his vision, his artistry and enterprise too, in large part are due the world-famed beautification of the Canadian side of the Niagara River and Falls, including extensive developments in Victoria Park, which were executed during his tenure as Chairman of the Niagara Parks Commission. He was the protagonist of the Hamilton Parks Board to whom primarily was due the Ambitious City's comprehensive parks improvement and extension program, including the acquisition of a large acreage of undeveloped land for a botanical garden. The Royal Botanical Gardens now cover 2,500 acres, the most extensive of its type in Canada. Here important research projects are being conducted in conjunction with the Ontario Research Foundation and McMaster University, in the beautiful landscaping of the campus of which he played a leading part. The last of the temporal honors to come to him was his selection, a week before his demise as Hamilton's "Man of the Year".

His fine historic perspective found an enduring expression in the restoration of such historic monuments in Ontario as Fort Henry at Kingston, the forts at Fort Erie and Queenston and Chief Jos. Brant's house near Burlington, now the Brant Museum. His practical bent found expression in providing Ontario with one of the most symmetrical systems of highways planned and partially developed in any major road building jurisdiction. In this he was fortunate in having as his chief lieutenant one of the world's greatest road engineers, R.M. Smith. During Mr. McQuesten's tenure as Minister for Ontario the high standard was established for the main travelled roads of northern Ontario which provided for them the same modern specifications in gradients, radii of curvature and sight distances which had been adopted for the King's Highways of southern Ontario. During his ministerial term, 1934–1943, approximately a fifth of a billion dollars was invested in *the roads and bridges of Ontario, the most important of the latter being the Rainbow Bridge at Niagara Falls. He envisioned a super-highway of the type of the Queen Elizabeth Way spanning the province from Windsor to the Quebec border and another linking it with the roads of Ontario's vast hinterland.*

Sir Christopher Wren, following the great fire of London in 1666, was the architect of many of the great buildings of the "Chief Citadel of Freedom", including approximately fifty of its churches, the greatest of which is St Paul's Cathedral. In it is the tomb of the greatest of Anglo-Saxon architects which bears a short simple epitaph in Latin which freely translated reads: "If you seek his monument, look about you". That epitaph is appropriately applicable in Ontario to Hon. T.B. McQuesten, whose presence graced many a meeting of the Ontario Motor League at the luncheons of which for years his brother, Rev. Calvin McQuesten, has pronounced the blessing. **Hail! and Farewell.**

"THE FORGOTTEN BUILDER" AND PARTISAN POLITICS

Unfortunately Partisan Politics is a "dirty word" and no one wants to admit that it happens at all levels of politics. I have found that when it is mentioned a heavy silence descends upon the room. It was Tom's nemesis, and if we look at the record we see how it happened for Tom. He was a Liberal and had been a close associate of Mitchell Hepburn in the 1930s. He tried to set up the Commissions (Highways and Bridges) so that they would endure in spite of which party was in control as the government. However, in 1943, Progressive Conservative Premier George A. Drew was elected and his Conservative party held Ontario for the next forty-two years.

There can be little doubt that this is the major reason that Thomas McQuesten has become known as the "the Forgotten Builder." The bias against him was political in nature, and attempts to expunge his record were deliberate, so that by the time that the Liberals returned to office with David Peterson (1985–90) so much time had elapsed that Tom and his exemplary record were easily forgotten. When Tom was forced to resign he lost his hold on the Highways Commission but continued as Niagara Bridge Commissioner.

It was not until 1988, when a Liberal Government reigned again, that the High Level Bridge was finally re-dedicated as the "Thomas B. McQuesten High Level Bridge." A series of letters trace McQuesten's defeat on the Highways Commission until Tom finally resigned; he wrote briefly in reply to Premier Drew's demand for resignation: *I resign herewith as Chairman and member of the Commission* [W-MCP7-1.150; May 20, 1944]. However, it was not until three months later, in August of 1944, that Drew accepted McQuesten's resignation. Only time and the sway of politics will tell what the future holds for the memory of McQuesten and his outstanding record of service to Ontario.

Thomas McQuesten entered hospital on December 24, 1947 for cancer surgery, and he died on January 13, 1948.

Many years earlier, while Tom was still at school, Ruby wrote to him as his mentor and muse, with a prophetic vision, and hoped that he would: *be a man able to separate between good and evil ... and as a lawyer to distinguish that faint line between right and wrong ... a man pure in politics ... and so strong that he would keep above the tide of wrong-doing and stand firm and help up others* [W-MCP2-4.053, May 8, 1905].

Thomas wrote to his mother : *I do know my dear mother that if I am going to achieve anything and come to you for commendation, I must come with clean hands.* Finally, Thomas was able to come to his sister, Ruby, and to his mother—***with clean hands*** [W5440, March 6, 1906].

Left: T.B. McQuesten and his mother Mary Baker McQuesten (Courtesy Whitehern)
Above: Thomas Baker relaxing in the gazebo in the Whitehern garden (Courtesy Whitehern)

Opposite page (top): Tennis at Whitehern (Courtesty Whitehern).
Opposite page (bottom): Hon. Thomas Baker McQuesten, working at his desk, which is now at the Royal Botanical Gardens, complete with inscribed brass plate (Courtesy Whitehern).

Victorian True Short Stories from the Whitehern Archives

*The Hon. Thomas Baker McQuesten, MPP.
Striding from the government buildings
(Courtesy Whitehern).*

THE END

www.ingramcontent.com/pod-product-compliance
Lightning Source LLC
Chambersburg PA
CBHW070904080526
44589CB00013B/1180